The New Pakistani Middle Class

AMMARA MAQSOOD

The New Pakistani Middle Class

Harvard University Press

CAMBRIDGE, MASSACHUSETTS, AND LONDON, ENGLAND   2017

Library of Congress Cataloging-in-Publication Data

Names: Maqsood, Ammara, 1983- author.
Title: The new Pakistani middle class / by Ammara Maqsood.
Description: Cambridge, Massachusetts : Harvard University Press, 2017. |
   Includes bibliographical references and index.
Identifiers: LCCN 2017013546 | ISBN 9780674280038
Subjects: LCSH: Middle class—Pakistan—Lahore. | Islamic renewal—Pakistan—
   Lahore. | Pakistan—Civilization—Western influences. | Pakistan—Civilization—
   Arab influences.
Classification: LCC HT690.P18 .M37 2017 | DDC 305.5/5095491/43—dc23
LC record available at https://lccn.loc.gov/2017013546

For Abbu (1941–2015)

jaise ṣaḥrā'on meṅ ćāle haule se bād-ĕ-nasīm
jaise bīmār ko be-wajhā ārām ā jā'iyē
  (Faiz 1943, *Naqsh-ĕ-faryādī*)

Contents

Note on Transliteration

Quotations from written and spoken sources are transliterated using John Thompson Platts's *A Dictionary of Urdū, Classical Hindī and English* (1884). All translations are my own. Speakers used Urdu, Punjabi, and English. English words that were used in otherwise Urdu and Punjabi sentences are placed in italics. For Urdu words and names commonly spelt and used in English, I have retained the local transliteration. For the sake of simplicity, commonly used Urdu plurals are indicated by adding *s* (for instance, *ḥijābs*, *'abāyahs*), except in those cases that would involve doubling of an *s*, in which case the broken plural is indicated (for instance, *majālis* instead of *majliss*). For the Quran, I have used Abdullah Yusuf Ali's (2008) translation unless specified otherwise.

The New Pakistani Middle Class

Introduction

"PAKISTAN IS JUST LIKE INDIA, except when it's just like Afghanistan," quip the writers of an article titled "How to Write about Pakistan" for the literary magazine *Granta*. As the authors remark, "It will become clear whether the Pakistan of our work is Indo-Pak or Af-Pak depending on whether the cover has paisley designs or bombs/minarets/menacing men in shalwar kameezes (there are no other kinds of men in shalwar kameezes)."[1] This article is, of course, satirical but it eloquently captures something about how Pakistan is represented and explained in a mass-mediated world. On the one hand, there is the imagery of terrorism and religious violence, a narrative that consistently appears in media and policy circles internationally, but is also amplified by a host of security experts, journalists, and think tanks within Pakistan. On the other hand, the authors also allude to aesthetic visuals associated with the Indian sub-continent. Here, Pakistan is celebrated through Mughal architecture, miniature paintings, and carpets (the paisleys the authors refer to), as well as the brightly colored truck art which features on the cover of this special *Granta* issue on Pakistan. Thus, one imagines a set of negative concep-tions, derived from violence and political instability, that link Pakistan to

Afghanistan and post-9/11 global concerns of terrorism. Offsetting this, a set of positive conceptions is introduced around creative expression and art, images that try to restore the country to its history within the Indian subcontinent. By positioning these narratives against each other, the article paints a binary vision of Pakistan and reveals the power of dominant images in our world and how they are constructed within and beyond the country.

The contest over pervasive images and definitions matters not simply in the realm of ideas and intellectual debate, but also because it shapes how particular groups struggle to get themselves legitimately recognized within complex social hierarchies and spaces. This book focuses on the way some of these images play out in the particular context of an expanding middle-class population in contemporary Lahore. It examines relations between an established middle class, composed of groups that yield significant social capital and have traditionally dominated urban life, and a new, more visibly religious, upwardly mobile middle class, one that has emerged in the last two decades. Through this focus, the book unravels how larger conceptions and accounts about the country inform the way these relations are mediated and how different middle-class groups present themselves to a world beyond Pakistan. My argument is preoccupied with a concern for understanding social recognition and upward mobility when set against the backdrop of a broader desire for modernity. As in other postcolonial countries, the lived experience of being middle class, especially in relation to the socioeconomic distinction that it affords, is closely tied to ideals about modernity. By considering growing trends in piety in upwardly mobile circles, this book sheds new light on the way these ideals are both aspired to, and contested, in the making of middle-class subjectivity. It is by no means a definitive account of all aspects of middle-class life in Lahore or urban Pakistan more broadly. Rather, the book probes how the politics of modernity meet the practices of piety in the struggle among different middle-class groups for social recognition and legitimacy.

This introduction offers an overview of the debates that I engage with in the forthcoming chapters, as well as provides a sense of the broader context of the ethnography. There are four main sections. The first section connects the history of modernism in the subcontinent to contemporary

forms of distinction and self-representation in Lahore. Through an explo-
ration of ongoing debates in the anthropology of Islam, the second section argues how new practices of piety in Lahore speak to the politics of
modernism and distinction. The third section provides a glimpse of the
fieldwork process, while also highlighting the need to consider the idea of
an imagined outside audience in the way different groups in Lahore
describe and represent their own practices and views. The final section
summarizes the main arguments of each chapter in the book. Throughout,
my aim has been to balance the ethnography with an accessible description of the wider sociopolitical context and relevant debates. In this sense,
I hope to address both an informed audience and those who have a scholarly interest in Pakistan, as well others concerned with the relations
between class, modernity, and religion.

MODERNISM AND THE MIDDLE CLASS

A central concern of this book is to unravel the ways in which a particular
history of modernism and representation of modernity continues to
mediate relations between middle-class groups. A historical context
serves as a useful starting pointing in understanding the linkages between
modernist ideologies and the middle class in postcolonial South Asia. It
is obvious, but often ignored, that groups comprising the middle class in
western Europe—where the term was first used—are different from those
that are typically considered as the middle class in the postcolonial world.
Dwyer tells us that references to people of "middling sorts" and of
"middle station" were common in late-seventeenth-century England, but
the term "middle class" first emerged in the late eighteenth century. In
other parts of Europe, the category "bourgeois" was used to describe this
group, but the word never gained prominence in English.[2] Moretti argues
that the indifference to the term here reflected the political environment and the establishment's desires for containment. Bourgeois groups
define themselves in opposition to established authority, such as nobility.
In England, where the early commercialization of agriculture had led to
de-feudalization and weakening of noble-bourgeois and urban-rural
distinctions, there was no significant use of the term "bourgeois."
Meanwhile, there was pressure—particularly from the political observers

of industrialism—for a middle rank that could act as an intermediary class between the rich and the multitude of poor workers. For the establishment, the term had a political purpose: "middle-class was a way to dismiss the bourgeoisie as an independent group, and instead look at it from above, entrusting it with a task of political containment."[3] The idea of the middle class was thus suffused with a sense of purpose.

Like contemporary uses, Dwyer argues that the term was hard to determine with definitions shaped as much by "what people are not" as by what they are. On the one hand, the category of middle class was used for people who were not part of the gentry, aristocracy, or the landowning groups and, therefore, were not individuals of independent means. On the other hand, such persons were also defined as not working class or laborers. "Middle-class" described

> those who worked but did not get their hands dirty, usually commercial or industrial capitalists with money from gift, inheritance, or loan with which they increased their capital. They employed those without money and who depended on others for their livelihoods ... so they were economically in the middle but had their own particular lifestyle and often shared a liberal individualism.[4]

Novels of the time offer an illustration of this emerging group. For instance, Jane Austen's fiction, written in the early nineteenth century, frequently mentions families that were not landed proprietors or from the working class but, instead, lived on interest from government bonds. Thus, in the context of the reconfiguration of the old social order, the rise of industrial capitalism, and the development of Enlightenment thought, a distinct English middle class began to materialize.

In late-eighteenth- and nineteenth-century colonial India, the term "middle class" began to be associated with indigenous professional groups, particularly government officials and bureaucrats, but also doctors, lawyers, and teachers (who were linked to the colonial state and public sphere). Thus it was state employment, rather than government bonds as in the case of their English counterparts, that facilitated the rise of an Indian middle class. At a broader level, the development of the Indian middle class dovetailed with larger changes in local registers of respectability and status. In conceptual terms, respectability in Muslim India was typically tied to descent from the Islamic heartland: *ashraf* families differentiated themselves from the *ajlaf* through claims of foreign origin. This distinction was conceptual rather than material—in practice, groups considered *ashraf* were not always of foreign origin—but it was one that equated respectability with descent.[5] During the nineteenth century, however, the virtue of achievement also began to appear as a marker of respect. Within this register, social standing did not come from birth, but through what one attained and did for others, a sense of self-discipline, and via philanthropy. Middle-class identity coalesced around this notion of respectability.[6]

Although the mind-set of the emerging middle class in India, with its emphasis on virtue and progressive improvement, was similar to its corresponding class in Britain, the social backgrounds of it members were not the same. The changing register of respectability drew families belonging to both old *ajlaf* and *ashraf* backgrounds. The colonial middle class thus consisted not only of traders and merchants—the classic "middling sorts"—from *ajlaf* families but also some of the landed gentry and those belonging to aristocratic backgrounds. The latter were particularly visible in high-ranking government and bureaucratic positions. They were, in this regard, "Macaulay's Children," the product of a colonial education policy that aimed to rid the Indian mind of "superstition" and to create a "class who may be interpreters between us and the millions we govern; a class of persons, Indian in blood and color, but English in taste, in opinions, in morals, and in intellect."[7] Members of this group were educated in colonial schools, and children of more affluent families were sent to universities in Britain, including Oxbridge and the London Inns of Court. Thus, older hierarchies did not completely disappear for it was often the older *ashraf* groups that formed the upper tier of the colonial middle class. This was, for instance, especially the case among Muslims in Punjab, where high-ranking government positions and gazetted honors had been bestowed upon landed Muslim families who had sided with the British in the 1857 war.[8] The middle and lower tiers of the colonial middle class—drawing from less-affluent *ashraf* and *ajlaf* groups—consisted of professional groups and nongazetted government officials.[9] In broader terms, however, state employment and participation in the colonial public sphere became a path toward middle-class respectability.

In 1947, after independence, it was the colonial middle class that took on the role of the nationalist bourgeoisie in the newly created states of India and Pakistan. While there is significant literature discussing the role of this national bourgeoisie in defining national culture in India, particularly during the Nehru years, there has, until recently, been comparatively little work on this subject for Pakistan.[10] As I argue in Chapter 1, in the late 1950s and 1960s, when General Ayub Khan was in power, national culture in Pakistan was inflected with *ashraf* etiquette and progressive sensibilities of the upper echelons of the middle class. The sense of progressivism within this class converged with the ideals of modernization theories, which enjoyed international support at the time, to produce a particular vision of modern urban life. This image served both as a model for aspiring middle-class groups and a promised national future of the teleological drive toward modernity. As recent work on left-wing activism has highlighted, this vision was bitterly contested and fraught with contradictions.[11] Even in Lahore, where a small middle class was able to develop and progress, largely through state employment and subsidies, Ayub Khan's policies faced significant opposition. By the end of the 1960s, when Ayub Khan was forced to resign following nationwide protests, this vision had not only failed in shaping a shared national culture but had also not delivered on its modernist promises.

This particular history of modernism, with its linkages to the colonial past and vision of a "modern" future, continues to be relevant in present-day Lahore. In particular, I argue that this history is evoked in mediating relations between what I define as an old and a new middle class. Broadly speaking, the old middle class consists of families and groups that progressed through state employment, and participation in the urban public sphere, during colonial rule and in the early decades after independence. It thus not only includes families that occupied high-ranking government positions in the newly created state, but also the emerging urban groups of the 1950s and 1960s that were able to utilize state support to progress to an established status. In most cases, the younger generation of these families is no longer linked to the state but is, instead, employed within the private sector. The new middle class consists of upwardly mobile urban groups that have emerged since the 1980s; many of them are second-generation migrants from smaller towns and rural areas in Punjab, while others are indigenous to the walled city and surrounding areas of

Lahore. Predominantly educated in government schools and colleges, many of them are employed in state institutions while a significant portion works in mid-level positions in the private sector or runs small businesses. Although some groups within this new middle class have some economic capital, most of them are vulnerable to setbacks, caused by sudden death or illness of the main earner, or by economic and political instability in the country.

As I underscore in this book, the boundaries between the old and new middle class are by no means fixed. Rather, they are produced and maintained by displaying attachment to, and familiarity with, the broader history of progressivism in the city, as well as in colonial South Asia more broadly. In Lahore, old middle-class groups distinguish themselves from newer groups through genealogical ties to well-known families and local notables of the past, many of whom were part of the colonial government or the newly created Pakistani state. More importantly, a link to the progressive past of Lahore is displayed through a habitus—that is, those tastes and sensibilities that display an affinity for the "lost" culture of the Lahore of the 1950s and 1960s. This includes exchange of stories, photos, and newspaper articles on life at this time, as well as participation in literary and cultural events that aim to revive the old social life of Lahore. Nostalgia for this past laments not only the end of that era but, more importantly, its imagined future of a "modern" Pakistan. It transforms into a moral claim, one that is directed at newer groups in the city for not sharing the "modern" sensibilities of the past. This nostalgia in local class politics dovetails with, and draws strength from, the larger national narrative through which Pakistan is often explained to the outside world—a country that was on its way to progress before being destroyed by the religious extremism that now grips the country. And it is often through this lens that old middle-class groups, as well as the outside world, understand the new forms of piety that are noticeable in new middle-class circles, a subject that this book also addresses.

ISLAMIC REVIVAL AND PIETY

New practices of piety, centered around the cultivation of individual ethics through a personal study of the Quran, reflect wider class tensions. In making this claim, I both engage with and enrich ongoing debates in the anthropology of Islam, while also shedding light on aspects where there is an overlap between academic sensibilities and popular portrayals within Pakistan. Since the turn of the century, there has been a steady growth in the number of Quran schools and religious study circles in Lahore. As noted elsewhere in the Muslim world, such schools and study circles are part of a broader move toward an acquired cultivation of individual ethics through understanding and studying the Quran.[12] Most of these schools do not follow any particular school of jurisprudence *(fiqh)* and, even those that do, tend to emphasize the need to build a direct and personal relationship with Allah through personal study and scholarship. This concept of reading the Quran with translation and commentary is not new but, until recently, it has not been a common practice among educated urban groups in Lahore. In Pakistan, as in other parts of the Muslim world, reading the Quran in Arabic takes precedence over reading it in local languages. The growing popularity of this practice is matched by an increasing presence of Islamic scholars and religious television programs, particularly talk shows on local channels. Like the Quran schools, many scholars and television shows highlight the relevance of Islamic ethics in contemporary middle-class life by pointing out its compatibility with rational and scientific discourses, and its ability to provide solutions for problems plaguing Pakistan in its drive for progress and stability. This kind of religious sensibility actively fosters and displays connections with a global Muslim community.

In Lahore, this shift toward personalized piety is most noticeable in the new middle class and among upwardly mobile groups. It is in these circles that religious study gatherings *(dars)* have become a common feature and there is a growing trend for women and men to attend Quran schools. In comparison with established groups there are more visible signs of religiosity in new middle-class groups. For instance, a significant number of women cover their hair or veil, often wearing a headscarf and *'abāyah*, whereas beards among men are not uncommon. This shift toward personalized piety has been accompanied by increased participation in a broader culture of religious consumption, which includes Islamic television programs, banking services, and veiling fashions, that both fosters and displays a global Muslim identity. Among established middle-class groups in Lahore, and within urban Pakistan more broadly, these trends are often viewed as a sign of the growing influence of Wahhabism—exported from Saudi Arabia.[13]

In this way of thinking, all kinds of old and new reform movements and groups are lumped together under the category of "Wahhabi" or "fundamentalist" and are often associated with religious and sectarian violence in the country. Frequently viewed as the consequence of the Islamization policies of General Zia-ul-Haq, the military dictator who ruled the country in the 1980s, the spread of Wahhabi Islam is condemned as destroying the tolerant and Sufi-inspired "authentic" Islam of Pakistan. At a broader level, among established urban groups, these trends of piety reflect a "historical failure," a faltering of the national drive toward the "telos of modernity."[14] This sense of the loss of a "modern" future, as I discuss in this book, often becomes a vehicle of distinction for old middle class families in Lahore. By aligning themselves with the modernist past of the region and bemoaning the present, established groups construct themselves as *khāndānī* and differentiate themselves from the new middle-class and upwardly mobile groups.

The wariness and, significantly, the disdain in established circles of Lahore for new forms of piety mirror some tendencies within academic discourse on Islam in South Asia. In particular, as Osella and Osella have highlighted, contemporary work on South Asian Islam often constructs a distinction between Sufism-derived popular Islam, represented as culturally specific, tolerant, and pluralistic, and reformist Islam, which is cast as foreign-inspired, closed, and rigid.[15] Such depictions are not only dismissive of the long history of homegrown Islamic reformism in South Asia, but also ignore the overlaps and engagement between Sufi and reform movements.[16] We are thus reminded not to treat "traditionalist" or "reformist" as "substantial categories but rather as produced discursively—and rhetorically—in the context of public debates."[17] In this context, recent anthropological work has paid attention to how debates between "traditionalists" and "reformists" lead to changes in practice, and how formal movements and laypeople alike reason, negotiate, and shift positions over time. Moreover, this work has emphasized that, rather than being rigid and closed, reformism opens up debate and creates possibilities for change and new interpretations.[18]

Against this backdrop, I argue that the trends of personalized piety in new middle-class groups are neither representative of growing

"Wahhabism" nor can be considered as an instance of "global" Islam eroding local registers of Muslim identity and process.[19] Following Osella and Osella's analysis of reformism in Kerala, I suggest that these trends need to be understood simultaneously as part of a "global Islamic impulse for purification and also as a deeply rooted and specific phenomenon, which produces itself through practice and dialogue."[20] On the one hand, appeals to a universal Islamic identity are common in new pious middle-class circles, as is a desire to remove cultural innovations from religious practice. Yet, on the other hand, new forms of piety are influenced by, and are mediated through, local concerns of progress and class mobility; moreover, they are grounded in an overall context where connections to the outside world are a mark of modernity.

In new middle-class and upwardly mobile circles in Lahore, a shift toward personalized piety is subsumed within a larger aspiration of "moving forward," both in terms of individual life-courses and in relation to the collective position of Pakistanis and Muslims more broadly. "Moving forward" thus encapsulates a desire for individual progress, marked by education, material prosperity, and upward mobility, and, simultaneously, a determination to use these resources to make a conscious effort to become a better Muslim. Here, understanding the reasons behind Islamic practices, through personal learning, emerges as a way of self-fashioning a modern Muslim identity, and of distancing oneself from "backward" and "traditional" practices. Such a conception of "moving forward" has similarities with Lara Deeb's description of modernity as material and spiritual progress in Shi'ite Beirut, as well as with Osella and Osella's view of Kerala's reformism "as index—via notions of education and progress—of a particular engagement with the modern."[21] More importantly, and, in this respect, distinctive from other studies, I unravel how these trends of personalized piety speak to, and are mediated by, class tensions in Lahore. Projects of Muslim self-fashioning in new middle-class circles contest the moral domination of established middle-class groups, while also being influenced by the modernism-inflected class rhetoric that otherwise casts them as "unmodern."

At the same time, concerns about being perceived as "backward" in the local class hierarchy often conflate with a broader sense of negative perceptions of Muslims in the West. In this respect, these projects of self-fashioning are also directed toward the wider world, with an intention of changing perceptions of the "backwardness" of Muslims by displaying a modern identity. Here, Muslims in the West, and the discourse of "global" Islam more broadly, are often cited as examples and as a general model to emulate but, in practice, this model is not followed uncritically. Rather, it is used as a site for debate and dialogue in relation to the specific needs of Pakistani Muslims, and the problems that they face in their aspirations for moving forward.[22]

By considering the wider environment in which new piety practices are taking ground in Lahore, this book also addresses the recent focus in the anthropology of Islam on individual experiences of ethical self-cultivation. It will be helpful here to briefly provide the context in which this scholarship has emerged. Much of the recent literature attempts to redress the normative assumptions in the academic work on Islam that emerged in the 1990s. Responding to the increased presence of Islam—both in relation to political movements and individual religious practices—this earlier body of work explained such a resurgence in relation to the larger social, economic, and political structures that motivate them.[23] Although these accounts provided a detailed understanding of the sociological base of new Islamic movements, they were often instrumentalist in their outlook and viewed emerging forms of piety as linked to identity politics or forms of economic and social acquisition.[24] Moreover, as its starting point, this body of work often took the absence of religion from the modern public sphere as normative, and then attempted to explain why this has not been the case in the Muslim world.[25] In doing so, it assumes not only the trajectory laid out in the modernization narrative but also displays an attachment to the broader values of and an imagined future within the liberal tradition. Recent anthropological work on individualized projects of pious, ethical self-cultivation—Saba Mahmood being a notable example—has attempted to separate itself from these normative biases and assumptions. Through an engagement with the personal desires, aims, and affects of followers of Islamic movements, ethnographies of ethical self-cultivation have highlighted the difference between conceptions of moral autonomy and agency in Islam and in the liberal tradition.[26]

Such work makes a key intervention in that it draws out the problems in analyzing pious subjectivities through normative liberal conceptions. In this way, it challenges instrumentalist perspectives by urging us to think of different forms of piety not as means to an end, but as agency in itself.[27] Yet, as important as this perspective is, its tendency to impose a singular focus on piety isolates this pursuit from other aspirations, obligations, and desires, while also obscuring the wider social and political environment. Although the intention is never as such, it tends to echo orientalist imaginings of Islamic tradition as unchanging and timeless—an image that leaders and adherents of religious movements also project. In considering wider class hierarchies, my intention is not to return to instrumentalist accounts, where religion is explained away as political or social gain. Rather, it is to emphasize that ideas on personalized piety in Lahore are "discursively produced" in conversation with competing religious discourses, as well as in relation to the "progressive" rationale of local class politics.[28] While others have critiqued the singular focus on the disciplinary power of piety movements for not considering the conflicting desires that govern everyday life, I argue that, in Lahore, emerging ideas on piety bring together a variety of aspirations.[29] In their emphasis on education, generalized rationalization, and scientific thinking, new forms of piety cater to the needs and disciplinary demands of middle-class life. However, we need to be cautious about understanding these trends through a Weberian trajectory of rationalization of religious practice. New ideas on piety not only coexist (sometimes uneasily) with ideas on transcendence but also, as I describe in Chapter 3, tend to "overstand," producing their own forms of "enchantment."

FIELDWORK AT "HOME" AND THE "OUTSIDE" WORLD

While debates on Islamic traditions among Muslims, outside of scholarly circles, have received significant attention in the literature on religious objectification, few have talked about the impact of discussions, or imagined dialogues, on Islam by non-Muslims. During my fieldwork in Lahore, conducted predominately in 2009–2010, this sense of how others perceive Muslims was pervasive. At the time, the country was experiencing a wave of violence, instigated by the Pakistani Taliban, an aftermath of the state's support of the United States–led invasion of Afghanistan. In Lahore alone, there were multiple deadly attacks in that year, including a devastating bombing at a market on the night before Eid al-Fitr that killed more than sixty people. The anxieties caused by the attacks, along with the general increase in sectarian violence over the last two decades, were frequently addressed in daily conversations.

More often than not, in such discussions there was an easy transition between what was happening in the country to how the world outside viewed Pakistan. In other words, problems within Pakistan were often articulated through anxieties about self-image. For instance, while talking about terrorism one informant said that "things are so bad that the moment there is a bomb blast anywhere in the world, everyone assumes that there must be some Pakistan connection."[30] Similarly, whether anyone outside remembers or not, Lahoris constantly recall to one another how *Newsweek* magazine once labeled the country "the most dangerous nation in the world."[31] Most felt that the increasing violence in their country simply confirmed the general opinion, across that world, that Muslims were "barbaric" and "uncivilized." The embarrassment arising from this coalesced with a broader awareness that Pakistan was viewed by others as a "backward" country, behind in the race for progress and marginal on the global stage. The idea of an imagined audience, an outsider that needs to be addressed and convinced otherwise, was a recurring feature of my fieldwork in Lahore. I draw upon this throughout this book, but it is also a sense in which I, as a native anthropologist, found myself deeply entangled.

When the fieldwork began, it was my intention to focus solely on the increasing prevalence of new forms of piety, to understand the motivations toward this shift and the ways in which it played out in individual lives. Yet, the more time that I spent with women from *dars* gatherings and their families, the more I realized how their ideas on piety spoke to a broader politics related to class and ideas on modernity in Lahore. The feeling that my informants were addressing an outside audience was a repeated occurrence and, especially during our initial meetings, was not purely accidental. Writing about his native Johannesburg, Jonny Steinberg reflects that when he "lock[s] eyes with a stranger, there is a flicker, a flash communication, so fast it is invisible, yet so laden that no words might describe it."[32] He continues, "Whoever he is, he clocks me as I pass, and reads me and my parents and my grandparents; and I, too, conjure, in an instant, the past from which he came." Fieldwork at home carried a similar familiarity, a connection between me and those I wanted to write about that predated our actual meeting.

I grew up in Lahore and attended a school and a liberal arts program at a local university that placed me in the social and intellectual circles associated with the kind of progressivism that, predominantly, views new religious trends as "inauthentic." Despite it never being addressed directly, it was a background that my informants were immediately aware of. In initial interactions, most people implicitly addressed the assumptions that came with such a background by articulating their position in relation to dominant ideas on what it means to be modern in Pakistan. This eased after a while, as we met more frequently, but then I acquired a different kind of role. I often felt that I was addressed as a spokesperson, someone now entrusted with the task of telling others (both locally and in the outside world), of the modernity of my informants and, more importantly, of their Islamic practices. It was, however, not only in conversations at *dars* gatherings or at Quran schools that I experienced the sense of being a spokesperson, or the presence of an imagined audience.

In established circles of Lahore, I was often asked about my research on Quran schools. Many of these questions and broader remarks reflected the assumptions that my informants at Quran schools had been so aware of. I was often asked, for instance, how we could stop this "Wahhabi brainwashing" or the notion that the people at Quran schools were all Taliban sympathizers. As I discuss in the first chapter, what was equally noticeable here was how this image of the urban masses moving "backward" was a way in which established groups constructed their own modernity, including with an outside audience as a constant presence. Due to these experiences, I broadened my focus and began to consider my initial questions through the lens of class, the intersection with local ideas on modernity, and the connections with perceptions of the world beyond Pakistan.

As mentioned, the bulk of this fieldwork was conducted in 2009–2010. From June 2009 to April 2010, over a period of eleven months, I was based in Lahore, along with shorter research periods in 2012 and 2013. During the longer period of fieldwork, I attended classes at a local Quran school for women, predominantly visited by young middle-class women.

I was fortunate that many of my classmates were happy to meet outside the school, and often introduced me to other friends and family members. In this way, I was able to extend my network of informants beyond the Quran school and came in contact with *dars* gatherings in different neighborhoods of Lahore. The classes at the Quran school primarily exposed me to the views of middle-class women, although I was later introduced to family members of both sexes. An opportunity to interact with different middle-class groups, both from established and upwardly mobile circles, came from part-time work as a focus group moderator at a local market research and advertisement company. I worked for the company for six months, and in that time I was able to freely interact with other male and female employees, most of whom came from a range of middle-class backgrounds. More importantly, being a focus group moderator meant that I was continuously meeting and talking to new participants, and often, our discussions would drift away from the product at hand to different topics. In addition to this, I participated in literary and cultural events, generally organized and attended by old middle-class and established groups.

Using the Quran school and associated *dars* gatherings as sites has meant that I was predominantly exposed to Sunnī views and ideas. Originally, I had hoped to include perspectives on piety from both sects and attempted to attend Shi'a gatherings. However, I later came to the conclusion that I did not have enough access to the latter and focused my ethnography on Sunnī perspectives. In order to maintain the privacy of my informants, I have used pseudonyms throughout this book. The only exception to this are interactions with individuals in prominent public positions or those who are locally well-known. In these cases, I felt that such individuals would be recognizable even if I withheld names.

PLAN OF THE BOOK

The first part of the book, covering Chapters 1 and 2, unravels the construction of the "modern" in postindependence Pakistan. It explores how such notions continue to influence relations between, and self-representation of, old and new middle-class groups. Chapter 1 dissects the nostalgia surrounding the early decades of Pakistan and within established and old middle-class circles in Lahore. In particular, it argues how nostalgia for the 1950s and 1960s transformed a class-specific experience of upward mobility and urban life in Lahore into a normative claim about modern life. The modernization programs of those decades were largely unsuccessful, and the broader specter of modernity constructed around them continues to have many afterlives. This is particularly the case in Lahore, the capital of the prosperous province of Punjab, where a small middle-class population was able to progress in the 1950s and 1960s with the help of government support. In present-day Lahore, the experiences of these groups, along with the established families of the time, are pitted against not only the violence and problems that now confront the country but also the conservatism and religious practices of new urban groups. Moreover, I argue that this transformation—nostalgia for a specific experience that morphs into a normative claim—is linked to broader politics of self-representation and cultural intimacy on a mass-mediated "global" stage.

Chapter 2 is concerned with relations between old and new middle-class groups in Lahore, a struggle for social differentiation that involves an overlap between class and moral rhetoric. By providing a description of the different groups that inhabit Lahore, I uncover how the modernist history plays into the ways in which old middle-class identities are constructed and in self-descriptions of growth, progress, and modernity within upwardly mobile groups. Moreover, in focusing on the varying rhetorical registers through which middle-class groups construct themselves as modern, I reveal how ideas on Islam and *asl* (real) Islamic practices exist within a broader moral economy of knowledge. Thus, I argue that ideas on Islamic practices reflect not only wider class politics but also the position of a person within the broader hierarchy. In this respect, I suggest that ideas on Islamic practices and on cultivating pious ethics cannot be considered outside of, or separate from, aspirations of upward mobility, progress, and the desire to be viewed as "modern."

The latter part of the book, covering Chapters 3 and 4, is concerned with piety practices in new middle-class and upwardly mobile groups, and how they are reflected in emerging patterns of religious consumption. Chapter 3 focuses on the increasing popularity of Quran schools and religious study circles among women in new middle-class groups in Lahore. While much of recent debate in the academic literature has focused on the outcome of projects of ethical self-cultivation, I choose to examine here how this desire is articulated and explained. In doing so, I draw out the variety of aspirations that coexist in the move toward developing a personal understanding of the Quran. I shed light on how the discipline and ethics promoted by this form of piety address some of the broader requirements of middle-class life. Moreover, this chapter depicts how ideas on piety are discursively constructed, partly in view of the demands and aspirations of middle-class life, but also in relation to broader perspectives on the West and Muslim life abroad. I argue that this form of piety, particularly its insistence on the compatibility of Islam with modern middle-class life, encourages rationalization in certain areas of religious practices but cannot be considered as part of a broader systemization. At the same time, I show how it simultaneously creates its own forms of "enchantment," often by encouraging an "overstanding" of Islam.

Chapter 4 revisits the connections and linkages between Islamic practices in Lahore and Muslim life in the West through the lens of religious consumption. It examines prevailing headscarf and veil fashions among upwardly mobile and new middle-class groups, as well as the increase in sales of Quranic storybooks, videos, and board games for children. I argue that the popularity of these goods in Lahore often rests upon their perceived popularity among the Muslim diaspora in the West. For instance, in relation to upwardly mobile women, I explore how headscarf fashions and tastes are often determined by what their relatives abroad are wearing, as well as through information gathered through private television channels and the Internet. Participating in these "global" trends allows these women to distance themselves from the "backwardness" associated with traditional veiling styles and to display a modern Muslim identity. At a broader level, the chapter focuses on the ways in which these patterns in religious consumption reflect an aspiration on the part of new middle-class groups to bypass the moral domination of the established groups in the local class hierarchy by attaching themselves to a larger abstract Muslim identity. The ethnography that follows is focused on Lahore— the local, so to speak—but it shows that beyond the immediate sociology of Pakistan and its recent history, there is a continuous sense of a global stage, where people struggle to define themselves in relation to an outside world.

ONE

Remembering a Modern Pakistan

LAHORE IS A CITY that beckons outsiders to its past. Many, of course, are inclined to do just that, having first encountered the city through the eyes of Rudyard Kipling's *Kim* (1901) or made familiar with its glorious Mughal past through historical work. Within the subcontinent, Lahore is often remembered as the lost heartland of a brutally partitioned Punjab. The collapse of this heterogeneous metropolis at Partition, encapsulated evocatively in Bapsi Sidhwa's *Ice Candy Man* (1988), evokes a sense of loss, particularly when compared to the religious homogeneity of present-day Lahore. At times, it seems as if the physical landscape too is determined to remind the observer of a lost time. Despite frequent attempts by the state to nationalize the names of roads and landmarks, which inevitably translates into "Islamize," older terms continue to thrive: Lakshmi Chowk, Guru Mangat Road, and Lawrence Gardens to name just three. Viewed from the "sepia-cultured lens" of this past, Lahore appears draped in a kind of melancholy akin to what the writer Orhan Pamük describes as the *huzün* that surrounds Istanbul.[1] It is, however, not just Lahore's position in the literary and historical imagination that sparks nostalgia. Lahoris themselves take pleasure in mourning their city. In their preference for memories of the city past to its present, Lahoris resemble the inhabitants of Maurilia, one of Italo Calvino's imaginary cities. Describing Maurilia and its people, he writes,

> If the traveller does not wish to disappoint the inhabitants, he must praise the postcard city and prefer it to the present one, though he must be careful to contain his regret at the changes within definite limits: admitting that the magnificence and prosperity of the metropolis Maurilia, when compared to the old, provincial Maurilia, cannot compensate for a certain lost grace, which, however, can be appreciated only now in old postcards, whereas before, when that provincial Maurilia was before one's eyes, one saw absolutely nothing graceful and would see it even less today, if Maurilia had remained unchanged.[2]

In Lahore, the glorious but now lost Mughal past, the dilapidated state of historic sites, and the indifference of the government to the city's heritage are all enduring topics of discussion. Longtime dwellers often lament that rapid growth and commercialization have destroyed the old-world charm of Lahore. In certain circles, the more recent past of the city is also a point of conversation. Here, it is common for the present to be compared (mournfully) with the Lahore of the 1950s and 1960s. I encountered this especially in the early days of my fieldwork, when I was frequently invited to cultural events, such as book launches, poetry recitations, drama performances, and musical evenings, all aimed at reviving the arts and literary scene in the city.

In those days, eager to meet people and build a contact base, I attended most of these events. I discovered at such gatherings that the organizers and attendees would regularly discuss a professed need to showcase and promote the "lost culture" of Lahore. Many would lament that this culture had been destroyed by the Wahhabi Islam that had been introduced by General Zia-ul-Haq, the military dictator who ruled the country in the 1980s and instituted a range of Islamization policies. What remained now, they claimed, was of little value. On hearing that I was a researcher based at a Western university, I would be urged to write about all that was being done to promote these lost traditions and arts. My reply—that I was interested in contemporary understandings of modernity—would be greeted with skepticism. "There is no modern to write about now, this is a country that has shunned modernity." Most of those gathered at these events were of the opinion that Pakistan had been more modern in the 1960s. At that time, this had been a young country, plagued by many problems, but one that was full of hope. As the organizer of a book launch (on Sufi shrines in Sindh) put it, "That was a time when we were on the right path, if our society had continued to move in that direction, we could have called Pakistan a truly modern country."[3]

Over time, I felt that there was a certain predictability to these gatherings. Whether it was an art gallery opening, an evening of *gazal,* or a book launch, I often met the same groups of people. Many of them, but certainly not all, had some connection to the political and cultural life of Lahore in the 1960s and 1970s. For instance, some of them had been (or were the offspring of) prominent government officials and industrialists of the time, while others were journalists, university teachers, or development workers who had started their careers at this time. Some of these individuals had progressed to become part of activist groups opposing the Islamization program launched by Zia. There was thus an inevitability to how the conversation invariably drifted toward the past along with a lament about the contemporary state of affairs. Neither the people nor the topics tended to change very much. This pattern became so familiar that such events began to appear to me like a rehearsal of some kind: the same faces, in the same roles, repeating the same dialogues. There was a staged quality to the events, where the conversation was directed not to each other but toward an uninitiated audience—an outsider, one might say—who had to be introduced to the "real" (lost) culture of the land. I often wondered if *I* had been cast as an outsider at these events. I am no stranger to Lahore, having lived in the metropolis for over two decades, but as someone writing about the city to an outside audience, it was as if I had been placed in such a category. Indeed, in the moments where particular concerns—often related to Islamization—were impressed upon me, the interaction had the feel of a foreigner being familiarized with the lie of the land. But if these instances were now mimetic of the classic encounter between outsider and local, my hosts too had acquired a position: the "authentic" bearers of culture.

This chapter considers how nostalgia for a particular period in Pakistan's history asserts a moral vision. In conjuring an image of a "lost modern," it constructs an ideal of urban life: what it once was and what it should be. Based on memories of city life in 1950s and 1960s, a time of Ayub Khan's state-led modernization, this vision derives largely from the experiences and aspirations of the small urban middle class of the time. It is thus a class-specific moral vision but, when deployed as a national narrative for the outside world, it transforms into a normative claim about modern life. Other morals visions, as we see in coming chapters, are formed in relation to this normative claim. Unraveling this slippage, from a specific experience to a general claim, paves the way for understanding competing moral visions and ideas on modernity. Equally, it allows for reflection on how specific moral claims gain legitimacy through the presence of an imagined outside audience and, following that, on broader issues of self-representation and cultural intimacy in a world that consists of mass-mediated global stages.

The relationship between nostalgia and modernity has received considerable academic interest. While nostalgia has often been perceived as a result of absence, the failure of modernity to deliver on its promises, more recent work has reframed it in context of a sense of loss.[4] Most notably, Esra Özyürek has drawn attention to the rise of "nostalgic modernity," arguing that, in Turkey, "contemporary Turkish modernists experience the present as the decay of a former modernity and have chosen as their model for repetition the Turkish past of the 1930s."[5] In the face of the growing presence of Islam in the public sphere, there has been surge in a nostalgia for Kemalism, the official ideology of the secular and modernist republic founded by Mustafa Kemal Atatürk (1881–1938). While Özyürek is concerned with the linkages between nostalgia and the broader privatization of politics, I focus here on the production of nostalgic modernity itself, the kind of audience it imagines and seeks, and its effect on competing moral claims and visions.

At first glance, Pakistan may seem an odd choice for a discussion on nostalgic modernity. There is little in the country's tumultuous history to suggest that there was a period that could be considered as a "lost modern." Like Turkey, Pakistan also underwent a modernization program during a military dictatorship, but it was neither as expansive nor that successful. General Ayub Khan's policies led to increased inequalities and exacerbated ethnic tensions; by the end of his rule, the country was facing a widespread separatist movement that, ultimately, led to the creation of Bangladesh in 1971. It thus appears strange to think of this period as a golden age within Pakistan. It is, however, important to remember that while at the national level Ayub's modernization program was largely unsuccessful, it did create some pockets of prosperity. In Lahore, where the urban middle-class population was relatively small, increased access to state employment and an expanding private sector provided space for upward mobility. A significant portion of these families was able to utilize these opportunities to become, within the course of a generation, part of the urban elite in Lahore. Their memories of the past, along with the recollections of other elite families, serve as the basis of nostalgic modernity in Pakistan.

Like all forms of remembrance, this nostalgia is formed through the present. During Ayub's rule, many of these middle-class groups in Lahore were critical of his policies, and some of them took part in the protests that eventually led to his resignation. In the present, however, faced with the specter of religious terrorism, and, more importantly, the rise of a new middle class that challenges their monopoly over space, most of the old middle-class families view the past favorably. As in the case of the imaginary Maurilia, it is Lahore's present that renders the past "with a certain lost grace"; it is in its afterlife that Ayub's era and associated ideals take on the air of a lost modern.[6] In this chapter, I explore this interrelation between the past, nostalgia, and the modern in four ways. First, I provide a brief history of Ayub's modernization programs. Second, I discuss a particular vision of ideal modern life and the citizen that was propagated and, third, how the politics of self-representation on a "global stage" has morphed it into a normative claim about modern life. The final section describes how Ayub's vision of the modern continues to be utilized by the military for its commercial interests.

MODERNIZATION AND ISLAM
UNDER A MILITARY GOVERNMENT

Although my focus here is the martial law of General Ayub Khan (1958–1969), it should be noted that most of his policies were a continuation of previous trends and predilections. The shift toward centralized power, concentrated in the hands of a military-bureaucratic oligarchy, alongside a reliance on technocratic modernism were the hallmark of Ayub's decade, but had a longer genealogy within post-Partition and colonial politics. Ethnography is said to lack historical depth; history, however, assumes temporal succession. Particular periods get taken up later and become mythical, remembered in isolation of events before and after. In drawing upon this period in Pakistan's history, I want to highlight its continuity with events before and, more importantly, use it as a starting point for a discussion on its various afterlives.

Within nationalist historiography, Ayub Khan's military rule is often hailed as the "decade of development," a golden period in the country's history. The years following Partition were chaotic, as the new state, with its limited administrative experience and machinery, struggled to deal with the heavy influx of refugees from across the border, accompanied by food shortages and rising prices.[7] Apart from basic service delivery, the government was also unable to resolve larger political issues. Jinnah, the leader of the Muslim League and the first governor-general of the country, died a year after Partition, before any political structure or constitution was decided. After his death, politicians and civil servants occupying senior posts in the administration were unable to reach a consensus on such questions, to the extent that for almost a decade after independence the country still did not have a constitution. Moreover, the senior administration was rife with disagreement; between 1947 and 1956, the country went through four different governors-general, none of whom came close to completing their five-year term. In 1958, against this backdrop, the military intervened to end what it called a state of disorder and confusion. Blaming politicians for the failures of the state, the military government promised Pakistanis that its quick action and efficiency in administration would bring progress and development. Talbot writes that General Ayub Khan's "demonizing of politicians" and "paternal solicitude" for the masses reflected Pakistan's inherited vice regal tradition.[8] Certainly, Ayub Khan belonged to an administrative class whose views on social improvement and progress were similar to their colonial predecessors. Educated at Aligarh Muslim University—known for its Islamic modernist tendencies—and later trained as a military officer at Sandhurst, Ayub Khan, like many other senior figures in the military and bureaucracy, believed that the masses had to be steered toward progress.[9]

During Ayub Khan's rule, the military's predilection for directed change dovetailed with the recommendations of modernization theories, which were popular in the West as well as in the developing world. Most such theories ascribed to the teleological idea that there existed "a common pattern of 'development,' defined by progress in technology, military and bureaucratic institutions, and [of] political and social structures."[10] Thus, "traditional" societies could be guided through the stages of development that the West went through to become "modern." With assistance from the United States and other foreign donors such as Japan and West Germany, the military government embarked on a series of modernization projects. These included economic policies promoting rapid industrial growth, especially private large-scale manufacturing and infrastructure development projects, such as the construction of large dams for hydroelectric power and for the expansion of irrigation.[11] By adhering to the broader trust in scientific knowledge, it was envisioned that a rationalist approach to urban planning would solve problems of housing and unregulated growth in the city. For this purpose, architects and planners associated with the modernist movement, such as Greek architect Constantinos Doxiadis, were hired to design housing settlements, national buildings, and, later on, the new capital, Islamabad.[12] The technocratic optimism of modernist architects like Doxiadis—his planning philosophy Ekistis, "the science of human settlements" rested on the notion that technology and rational planning could "manage away" problems—dovetailed with the modernizing aims and aspirations of young postcolonial nations like Pakistan. The city, rationally planned, and inhabited by citizens who would reflect these progressive values, emerged as the archetype of the modern.

The presence of modernist experts and architects in Pakistan also helped convey, both locally and to the wider world, the modern ethos and international connections of the military rulers. At the time, the more popular modernization theories had created a group of experts and consultants who traveled to different parts of the developing world to implement similar projects for economic or agricultural reforms or provide models for urban expansion. An urban planner introducing a scheme for development in Baghdad one month would offer the same plan to Islamabad the next month and to another city in the month following.[13] Progress thus became closely intermingled with a sense of internationalism. In the postcolonial context, where connections to the outside world are a source of prestige, being part of this internationalism, even if peripherally, became a symbol of the state's strength and power. At the same time, it was viewed as a way to assert Pakistan's presence on the global stage. Malik notes that national buildings, constructed in the 1960s, represent a roll call for international "signature architects" of the period.[14] For instance, Robert Johnson-Marshall, a renowned modernist architect from Britain, planned the layout of the administrative sector of Islamabad and also designed the National Museum and National Arts Gallery. Japanese modernist Kenzō Tange designed the Supreme Court of Pakistan.

While the new buildings symbolized the modern ethos of the nation and the optimism of Pakistan's march toward progress, the military rulers simultaneously felt that they should reflect the unique character of Pakistani society on the international stage. For this reason, modernist architects were often asked to incorporate "Islamic" aspects in their designs, a demand that was not always accepted. These concerns were visible in the debate surrounding the selection of the design for the National Assembly building. The planning committee for the building envisioned it as a structure of "substantial size . . . and architecturally impressive" and "carefully designed to reflect the past culture, at the same time utilizing the modern methods."[15] Foreign architects associated with the modernist movement in architecture were commissioned but their plans were repeatedly rejected for not sufficiently reflecting the Islamic character of the nation. The first outside architect hired, Arne Jacobsen, refused to change his design, and was replaced by Louis Kahn, whose designs were also rejected for being "too foreign." The design selected in the end, by Edward Durrell Stone, was accepted for including features from Mughal architecture, in particular, the use of white marble façades.[16]

The use of "Islamic" features in modernist designs was representative of a wider appeal by the military government to, what Dale Eickelman calls, a "generic Islam."[17] Such a vision of Islam centers around the assumed universals—the five pillars—of the tradition, and underplays internal differences and regional specificities to construct Muslim life as similar everywhere. In the context of Pakistan, generic Islam served as an encompassing category that provided the nation with a unifying identity. On the international stage, it gave Pakistan a distinct identity that both distinguished it from other postcolonial nations and allowed it to participate in a broader Muslim world. At the national level, a state-centric generic Islam was used to hold the different ethnic factions together, a point I return to in the next section, while inculcating modernist values promoted by the state. As Paul Dresch noted of generic Sunnism, the "new" Islam of 1980s Yemen, state-centric Islam in Pakistan appropriated elements from different Islamic traditions that were compatible with goals of national consolidation and development.[18]

During his time in power, Ayub was often compared to the Turkish general and state modernizer Mustafa Kemal Atatürk, a comparison that must have pleased Ayub Khan as he was an admirer of the Turkish military's reformist agenda. Indeed, as discussed later in this chapter, the Pakistani military still likes to think of itself as similar to its Turkish counterparts although, as Lieven mentions, it has never successfully implemented a reform agenda like Atatürk's.[19] Unlike Atatürk, Ayub's agenda for modernization did not involve a complete separation of religion from public life. Rather, it drew upon generic Islam as a source of legitimacy and to inculcate "modern" sensibilities among the masses. This involved taking power away from traditional religious leaders, such as the *ulamā* and Sufis, and to center religious life around the state. To this end, Ayub tried to reduce the power of these leaders by bringing mosques and Sufi shrines under state control, transforming them from "religious" to "national" sites, a symbol of the generic Muslim identity and culture of Pakistan. In order to inculcate progressive values, laws such as the Muslim Family Laws Ordinance (1961) were introduced, which aimed to improve the status of women by changing existing laws and customs on divorce, polygamy, inheritance, and child marriages. The ordinance attempted to further sideline the *ulamā* as it allowed state officials to officiate marriage and divorces.

It is not just the national buildings of the time that reflect this vision of a state-centric generic Islam, but also the mosques that were constructed. During the 1960s, the mosques built by the military were tall structures with sharp modernist designs, characteristics that it associated with its own scientific and rational prowess. Often built with the latest materials and techniques in construction, they were designed to draw attention to the modern ethos of the military rulers. Moreover, they reflected an appeal to a wider sense of internationalism, coupled with a broader generic Muslim identity. This was visible, for instance, in the selection process and design of the national mosque in Islamabad. Doxiadis, the architect of the master plan for Islamabad, had intended that the capital's central mosque be built in the foothills of the Margalla Hills. In 1966, funding was secured from King Faisal, the monarch of Saudi Arabia, and the plan was selected through an international competition held in 1968 with the collaboration of the International Union of Architects. The winning design was submitted by the Turkish architect Vedat Dalokay who envisaged the mosque as an eight-sided concrete shell with minarets placed at four corners.[20] In a personal interview, an official who had been part of the selection process explained why the design had appealed to the committee:

> The idea was to have a grand mosque that symbolized the aspirations of the nation. We wanted to show that we are progressive, we do not hold on to tradition, we can innovate but still have religion in our society ... so we can build new and interesting things but that at our heart we are still Muslim. This mosque was like that, it was a progressive and modern design but it was still a mosque ... a place for us Muslims to pray together.[21]

The official's views here on the mosque eloquently capture the state's vision of Islam: it should be progressive and modern while bringing the whole nation together, but with the right amount of "tradition." Other architects and conversationalists that I spoke to in Lahore were skeptical if this had been the only reason that the design was selected. Although they agreed that much of the architecture of the time propagated the wider modernist ethos of the state, they believed that personal self-fashioning also accounted for the selection of Dalokay's design. They claimed that the committee, composed predominantly of army officials, liked the design because it was Turkish, and "every general in this country likes to think he is Mustafa Kamal Atatürk."[22]

The modernization program launched by General Ayub Khan was only partially—if it all—successful. The economic policies, based on the model of functional inequality promoted by modernization experts, led to the concentration of wealth among a tiny elite, and exacerbated regional inequalities. Under the model, it was assumed that wealth would eventually trickle down from elite groups to all classes. However, prosperity never trickled down widely and, when it did, it was predominantly in Punjab and among Muhajir groups in Karachi. Similarly, agrarian reforms initiated by Ayub Khan—the so-called green revolution—were largely limited to the rural heartland of Punjab. Economic prosperity among these groups, discussed in more detail shortly, came at the expense of other provinces and ethnic groups. By the late 1960s, wealth was largely concentrated within a tiny elite: just twenty-two families owned 66 percent of the nation's industry, 80 percent of the banking sector, and 97 percent of its insurance companies.[23] Meanwhile, the professional classes, such as doctors and teachers, as well as laborers and small farmers, were left to bear the burdens of rapid economic growth. Rising prices for industrial goods and food were matched by a decline in workers' wages. The rationalist city development plans were unable to cope with the rapid urbanization, nor were they able to prevent unregulated growth. The religious reforms too were met with resistance from religious parties and the 'ulamā. Many of these religious groups joined in the mass student and labor union protests against state elitism that were ultimately successful in removing Ayub from power in 1969.

Despite its failure to deliver on its promises, the modernization ideology propagated by Ayub has continued to influence national institutions and their policies. Akhtar, for instance, has highlighted how the technocratic approach to water management, adopted during the Ayub years, continues to dominate the national debate on water. Similarly, within the bureaucracy, there remains a strong reliance on science and technology to manage problems alongside a dismissal of politics as messy and unpredictable.[24] It is, however, not just the broader ideology that continues to persist. The military regime established a particular spectacle of modernity that has had various afterlives beyond and, outside of, its founding moment in the

Ayub years. The promise of science and rationality, the prestige afforded by international connections, and the desire for order and efficiency—these were the visions on which the "modern" in Ayub's time was constructed. In the coming chapters, I unravel the continued relevance of some of these visions, how they reappear in different forms, and role that they play in current contestations of modernity in Pakistan.

A "MODERN" URBAN CITIZEN

My main concern here, however, is the contemporary presence of a cultural ideal, closely linked to Ayub's modernizing vision, and its relationship with the nostalgic reminiscences that one encounters frequently in contemporary Lahore. As mentioned earlier, within the larger teleological ethos of progress, the urban became the ideal site of modern life, complete with the "promise of emancipated lifestyles and bourgeoisie pleasures (the cars, the lifestyle, marriage by choice)."[25] In the 1960s, the ideal citizen that inhabited this space emerged as a subject who inculcated progressive values, aspired to consume the bourgeoisie pleasures the city offered, but at the same time, was also steeped in a particular kind of North Indian aristocratic culture and form of comportment. National life and cultural representations of the time were dominated by the presence of UP-Urdu (United Provinces are considered as the heartland of courtly Urdu). In state-sponsored literary and cinematic representations, the ideal inhabitant was not only committed to a modernist worldview—depicted through Westernized mannerisms—but also possessed fluency in UP-Urdu and *adab*.

The propagation of Urdu in national life has often been read as an attempt to resolve deeper tensions within Muslim nationalism in South Asia. Historians have noted that at the heart of the struggle for Pakistan, there was a contradiction between the transcendental Muslim identity that the movement aspired to and the particularistic attachments—to locality and language—of the people who came under its umbrella.[26] It has been argued that that the particularistic identities of the groups within the territory have been countered through the promotion of an ideology of sameness: one religion (Islam), one language (Urdu), and one nation (Pakistan).[27] During Ayub Khan's rule, this sense of sameness was

propagated by the state and, often, by sponsoring a nationalist intelligentsia. The ascendancy of UP-Urdu was also reflective of the social composition of state officialdom and the bureaucracy. Urdu-speaking refugees
from India and, in particular, those from United Provinces, along with
Punjabis, were overrepresented. Senior positions in the government were
often occupied by bureaucrats originating from UP, many of whom had
previously been employed within the colonial state. In the 1960s, however, UP-Urdu became a general marker of elite life, and was associated
with groups that did not always come from Urdu speaking backgrounds
but had a stake in preserving the state.[28] In Sindh, the cultural hegemony
of Urdu was supported by Karachi-based industrialists, many of whom
were originally from Bombay and of Gujarati origin, who had been
beneficiaries of Ayub's economic policies. Equally, support for an Urdu-
oriented national culture came from the Punjabi senior bureaucracy and
army officials.

While I agree that the state propagated this cultural ideal—which tied
together modernist aspirations with UP-Urdu *adab*—I argue that it also
important to consider the deeper histories and relations that, perhaps
inadvertently, promoted it. Let me elaborate on the pervasiveness of this
ideal through a discussion of the opposition to Ayub's policies. Recent
academic work has highlighted the role of left-wing groups in challenging
the centrist tendencies and elite-centric politics that were taking root
in the nascent state.[29] Much of this work is centered on left-wing literary
activism in the first decade and a half after Partition and, in particular,
the works of writers associated with the All Pakistan Progressive
Writers Association (APPWA). The association was closely linked to the
Communist Party of Pakistan and, together, both groups launched a
severe critique of elite politics and its exclusionary nature. Given their
critical stance, and the broader context of Cold War geopolitics in which
Pakistan was aligned with the United States, left-wing groups were suppressed by the state—the Communist Party, for instance, was banned in
1954. By the time, Ayub came to power, most of these groups had been
dismantled or gone underground. However, the larger tradition of left-
wing activism was central in the protests that brought together students,
trade unionists, and members of the intelligentsia and were, ultimately,
successful in ending Ayub's martial law. Although this body of work has

highlighted the ways in which left-wing groups opposed state policies, it has, broadly speaking, underestimated how many of these writers and activists, in terms of their sociological background, inhabited many of the cultural ideals that were being promoted by the state.

Like many senior members and supporters of the establishment, prominent left-wing writers and communist activists belonged to privileged Urdu-speaking backgrounds. In this respect, they were very much part of the social milieu that historian Hamza Alavi termed the "salariat" (salaried groups). He writes that in colonial India, the "salariat" were "sons of Muslim *ashraf*" who maintained an "organic link" with landed groups, but were predominantly employed by the state.[30] For instance, the All India Progressive Writers Association—writers from it formed AIPWA after migrating to Pakistan at partition—was formed in 1934 in Oxford by a group of Indian students who were inspired by Marxism. Given their involvement with the state, these groups were very much part of the of the colonial middle class. Most of them were educated in colonial schools and colleges, and the children of more affluent families were sent to universities in Britain.

This shared background is visible in Kamran Asdar Ali's recent work on Pakistani communists in which he has highlighted the enduring friendships and family connections between these left-wing activists and high-ranking state officials. He notes, for instance, that in the early years after Partition, a period when the state was clamping down on Communist Party members, many were willingly hidden and protected by family and friends who were part of the establishment.[31] In drawing attention to these linkages, my aim is not to undermine the integrity and vision of left-wing activists and Communist Party workers. Despite their privileged backgrounds, many of them lived a basic existence without appeal to material prosperity.[32] At the same time, I do not want to belittle their resolve and commitment to forming a more equitable Pakistan. Rather, my intention is to blur the (often sharply imagined) boundaries between the state and civil society of this time. National life in Pakistan's early decades—whether it was informed by the state or its critics—was dominated by people who came from a similar background and were well-versed in the style of comportment emblematic of North Indian Urdu-speaking communities. Although they stood at opposite ends of

the political spectrum in certain respects, both groups shared between
them a teleological vision of progress in which religion, outside of its
functionality in modernizing, had no place in the public sphere. As
writers, poets, and public intellectuals, their work had a reach that
extended beyond their politics. The broader literary and cultural world
that they formed and informed reflected their Urdu-speaking background
and their commitment to that teleological progress.

The tying together of modernist aspirations with a particular cultural
form thus was not a result of state policy alone but linked left-wing
writers and the establishment in the promotion of a broader agenda.
Lahore was at the center, where both state discourses and left-wing literary activism came together to promote this broader cultural ideal. Many
of the writers, poets, and playwrights who had migrated from India at
partition had settled in Lahore. Here, they were joined by other Punjabi
writers who wrote primarily in Urdu. Irrespective of whether these writers
were sympathetic to the state's vision or were engaged in left-wing activism,
they together established a literary tradition in Lahore that was dominated
by Urdu. Many left-wing writers and intellectuals lived in middle-class
areas, such as the low-cost housing scheme Samanabad (discussed in the
next chapter), where they inspired and interacted with college students
living in the area.[33] The position of Urdu in cultural life was also bolstered
by the presence of high-ranking bureaucrats and state officials from Urdu-
speaking backgrounds.[34]Although Lahore was predominantly composed
of Punjabis, Urdu came to symbolize modern urban life.[35]

At the same time, the larger teleological model of progress held particular appeal in Lahore because it did, within the context of a small middle
class, live up to its promise. In Punjab, similar to other places, wealth was
concentrated within a small elite, but here, unlike other provinces, it did
"trickle down" to some extent. It was the province that had benefited the
most—and often at the expense of others—from Ayub's policies, and this
was apparent in the opportunities for upward mobility that were available
for aspiring groups in Lahore. Government scholarships and subsidies
allowed young people from middle-class areas, such as Samanabad, to
study in local colleges and universities. After graduating, many of them
were employed by the state, either within the bureaucracy, or as or as doctors, engineers, and university lecturers and teachers in government-run

institutions. Others found employment within the growing industry of
infrastructure development. This was also a time when, spurred by the
dictum of modernization theories, Americanized professions of private
sector corporate work and advertising were on the rise, providing further
prospects of upward mobility.[36] As I detail in Chapter 2, within a course
of a generation, many of these families were able to move to the elite
residential areas of Gulberg and Model Town, and along with the established elite, came to dominate public and cultural life in Lahore.

Although the middle-class groups described above benefited from
Ayub's policies in the long term, during his time in power, many of them
were critical of the rule. A significant portion participated in student
demonstrations while many others were sympathetic to left-wing groups
and their critique of state policies. Despite embracing some of the values
promoted by the state, the urban middle class was not uncritical of its
larger cultural agenda and the urban ideal that it promoted. The debates
between left-wing activists and pro-establishment writers, and, later on,
religious thinkers highlight how national culture was a contested category. This ongoing dialogue between different sides and, indeed, the
debates internal to each group, was very much part of the middle-class
milieu of the time.[37] However, in the present, where it is pitted against
overt religiosity in the public sphere, the past has become "sanitized" from
these contestations.[38] Within the reconfigured battle lines of the present—
between liberal and religious groups—the past is devoid of the politics
surrounding it, and is remembered for its broader progressive ethos. At
cultural events in concerts in Lahore, the works of left-wing literary
activists are often celebrated and showcased—Faiz Ahmad Faiz's *gazal*
being a prominent example—but they now serve as cultural symbols of a
lost "golden past." Through them, the people in attendance relive a time
when artists and activists were concerned with building a progressive and
forward-thinking society, the place of religion was firmly in the private
sphere, and when Pakistan could be proud of its international reputation.
It is in these moments, in the present, that Ayub's urban ideal exists in its
purest form.

Nostalgia, here, reconfigures; it transforms events, writings, and memories to construct a past that perhaps never existed, except as a contested
ideal. At the same time, nostalgia serves another purpose, one of social

distinction and differentiation. As the next chapter shows, being well-versed in particular literary styles and poetry and familiarity with urban life in the 1950s and 1960s are an integral part of the rhetorical strategies through which the old middle class differentiates itself from newer urban groups.

The moral vision that this nostalgia promotes gains its legitimacy from the larger audience that it aims to address and engage with. In Lahore, nostalgic reminiscences are linked to local contestations, but they are often performed with an "outside" audience in mind. It is this sense of being seen on a global stage that provides nostalgic narratives with authority, turning a class-specific experience of the past into normative claim. It is the discussion of this slippage, and its dependence on the presence of and connections to the outside world, that I now consider.

INTIMACY AND THE IMAGINED OUTSIDER

My initial months of fieldwork are reflective of a more general approach to conducting fieldwork in postcolonial cities, where academic access is usually brokered by local activists and development workers or by public intellectuals and journalists. Faced with the daunting prospect of identifying and meeting informants in large and unfamiliar urban centers—Lahore, for instance has over 9 million inhabitants—researchers understandably rely on such people to point them in the right direction. Often, the brokers of access are themselves involved in different kinds of social activism and there is an expectation that other researchers will lend their support, and become a part of that larger struggle. This holds true especially for the subcontinent, where there is a long-standing association between academia and activism for what are seen as "progressive causes." Moreover, like in other postcolonial states, connections to the outside world remain a source of status and prestige at the local level. And typically in Lahore, the people who broker access for researchers are those who are part of the old middle-class groups or at least identify with the ideals and narrative of that larger milieu. The areas of research that one is directed to, in this context, are those that are aligned with the broader goal of resisting the ascendancy of right-wing religious groups, many of which are seen as promoting militancy and violence. Public activism of this kind is not without its danger in Pakistan, and vocal critics of militant religious groups and of the state's policy to protect them are routinely harassed and, sometimes, killed. In such circumstances, the uneasiness that one feels at not lending support to the cause is matched by a reluctance to reveal the politics (or lack thereof) that may lurk beneath what are otherwise worthy projects. This often leads to the kind of "ethnographic refusal" that Ortner has noted of anthropological studies focusing on resistance.[39]

There are, however, other reasons for this type of ethnographic refusal that are related to deeper politics of cultural intimacy and national display. Self-representation, within a mass-mediated culture, hinges on the construction of social identities intended for display. Drawing upon Herzfeld's work on cultural intimacy, the idea that there are aspects of identity which are a source of external embarrassment but, at the same time, form a sign of commonality, Shryock notes that the idea of an imagined outsider is central to such forms of representation.[40] Cultural intimacy, he argues, internalizes and "renders essential the presence of an outside observer whose disapproval matters, whose judgment can be predicted, and (most important of all) whose opinion is vital in determining what value common sociality can have."[41] At the heart of the nostalgia there lies not only a sense of bewilderment and mourning at what has happened to the country in recent decades, but also a sense of embarrassment at how it is viewed by others. Most Pakistanis are painfully aware of how they are viewed by the world outside; they are perceived as a country of terrorists or, at best, backward religious zealots. It was this consciousness, of an outside audience that had to be convinced otherwise, that gave the cultural events the staged feel that I earlier described.

Like all other forms of display, self-representation is a kind of theater that involves a set of actors who speak on behalf of the community, an audience that watches them, and a stage. In other words, self-representation brings a set of insiders (actors) and outsiders (audience) together within a particular frame of reference. Within urban Pakistan, more broadly, the sense that there is an outside world that views the country negatively is central to cultural intimacy and to self-representation. It was out of the same feeling of embarrassment that I would often be encouraged to write about the efforts that were being made to revive literary and artistic traditions. Many of the organizers and participants at such events had a performative aspect. At a time when Pakistan continuously received bad press abroad, they believed that such events were a way to showcase aspects of their culture that need to be celebrated and promoted. Indeed, one could argue that these events are part of a broader trend, noticeable in urban Pakistan, to direct attention toward facets of local life and history that many believe serve as a counterpoint to the religious violence that plagues the country. For instance, alongside the cultural events described earlier, this includes an increased emphasis on the pluralistic Sufi traditions of the region, initiatives that publicize historical monuments and the natural beauty of the country, and campaigns supporting traditional handicrafts and artisanal work.

Nostalgic reminisces also weave their way into these larger displays of identity. Photos from Pakistan's early years—presented as a time when Pakistan enjoyed a favorable international reputation—are published in newspapers and exchanged over social media. Most of these images are from the 1960s and 1970s and depict scenes from urban public life, such as film billboards outside cinemas, newspaper advertisements, popular cafés and clubs, photos of local celebrities, and visits by foreign dignitaries. The same sense of mourning evident in the conversations at literary gatherings is found in the narratives surrounding such photos. A popular series of photo essays titled "Also Pakistan," published in the English-language daily *Dawn,* serve as an example. The essays consist of rare photos that the columnist describes as belonging to a time before Pakistan became a "quasi-Orwellian 'Islamist' dictatorship." The writer comments that "there is very little memory left of a *[sic]* Pakistan that today seems like an alien planet."[42] The "Also Pakistan" series also conveys the sense of internationalism that, in the urban imagination, is often associated with the 1950s and 1960s. For instance, one photo in the compilation is of Dizzy Gillespie playing his saxophone alongside a local snake charmer, and another shows Ava Gardner and Stewart Granger arriving in Lahore to shoot the film *Bhowani Junction* (1956). Another image is of Che Guevara in Pakistan on an official visit. The series include an old press advertisement of Pakistan International Airlines (PIA), the national carrier, featuring an image of the American comedian Bob Hope. There is also a photo of Jacqueline Kennedy at Heathrow

Airport, walking down from a PIA plane with the flight crew in attendance. The photographs serve as a reminder of the position Pakistan once had in the wider world.

The need to promote aspects of national culture that can improve Pakistan's image in the eyes of this imagined Western audience implicates what Richard Wilks calls the "the global structures of common difference," which "puts diversity on a common frame, and scales it along a limited number of dimensions, celebrating some kinds of difference and submerging others."[43] This global frame affects not only the social identities that anthropologists typically study, but also their own research parameters and choices. For instance, as someone familiar with Lahore, I am aware that many of the people who proudly claim Sufism as the "authentic" Islam of the country would shy away from being associated with—let alone showcase—some of its popular observances, such as visitations from dead saints or spirit possession. The poetry and aesthetics surrounding Sufism and its broader message of religious harmony are differences that can be celebrated on a global stage, while other sides of these tradition are *too* different to be shared. However, when faced with an unfamiliar audience, I too feel hesitant sharing this information and often stick to the usual story of the importance of Sufism in the region. Like their informants, most anthropologists also operate on global stages and are very aware of the kind of assumptions that an unfamiliar audience has about the area they study.

Like the title of the photo essays, projects and campaigns highlighting the positive aspects of the country are often labeled or discussed as examples of the "other Pakistan." In recent years, this side of the country has also received coverage in the international media. Foreign journalists and writers wishing to write on topics other than security concerns often focus on the kinds of events and happenings that "other Pakistan" discourse revolves around, including Sufi music, art exhibitions, and literary events. Matching the mood of the local press and activists, the celebratory note of the coverage is juxtaposed with the ever-present specter of religious violence. For instance, BBC News reported on the recent Lahore Literature Festival with the title "Book Lovers Defy the Bombers" and *The Guardian*'s coverage of the Karachi Literature Festival included a remark on how "books are really a matter of life and death."[44] Such portrayals not only draw upon a sense of loss but also speak within the wider narrative that holds Zia and Wahhabi Islam responsible for the problems that Pakistan now faces. Consider, for instance, the *New York Times* article titled "Mystical Islam Suits Sufis in Pakistan." It notes that "to this day Sufi shrines stand out in Islam for allowing women free access," before quickly moving on to highlight the dangers that the tradition faces now faces.

> In modern times, Pakistan's Sufis have been challenged by a stricter form of Islam that dominates in Saudi Arabia. That orthodox, often political Islam was encouraged in Pakistan in the 1980s by the American-supported dictator, Muhammad Zia ul-Haq. Since then, the fundamentalists' aggressive stance has tended to eclipse that of their moderate kin, whose shrines and processions have become targets in the war here.[45]

In the post-9/11 context, such accounts of Pakistan have become increasingly popular, and serve as both a support for and as a critique of the United States' war on terror. The disastrous consequences of U.S. involvement in the region and backing Zia during the Cold War are often cited as reasons for why it should not intervene again. Conversely, from the other side, the religious violence resulting from the Cold War agenda gives the United States the responsibility to act in the region in order to resolve these problems. Such representations mean that, both at home and abroad, Zia's Islamization regime and its dire effects have increasingly become the dominant frame for understanding and explaining contemporary Pakistan. Alongside this, the positive aspects of the country—the "other" Pakistan—are framed within a larger discourse of resistance.

My aim here is not to question the validity of this narrative; there is enough evidence confirming that Zia's policies have significantly contributed to Pakistan's current problems with militancy. Rather it is to consider the nostalgia that surrounds this narrative, and the reluctance—the "ethnographic refusal"—to consider the politics internal to these constructions. The mourning and nostalgia that surrounds conversations about Zia evokes an ideal of how things once were and what they should be like. The memories and imagery that it draws upon, however, are based on a class-specific experience of urban life. When presented as part of a national narrative—an explanation for the outside world—the particular moral vision becomes a normative claim about modern life.

THE "NEW" MODERN OF THE MILITARY

Just as narratives for an outside audience draw upon ideas and images of modern life from the 1950s and 1960s, the Pakistan military also depends on this history to justify and further entrench its dominant position in the country. Not only does its image—established in the Ayub years—as the only efficient and modern institution in the country legitimize its presence in national politics, it also serves its expansive economic interests. Alongside its continuing involvement in civic infrastructure and transport development, the Pakistani military owns thousands of acres of farmland and runs nationwide insurance companies and banks, as well as food industries.[46] In addition to this, the army is firmly positioned in the urban real-estate market, and owns housing societies, called Defence Housing Authority (DHA) or Askari Housing, throughout the country. It is here that the enduring legacy of the spectacles of modernity of Ayub Khan's rule are most powerfully reflected. Much of the success of the DHA, as I show in this section, draws upon Ayub's vision of modern life but transforms it from an ideal of collective progress to a marker of individual success.

As is the case in other cities in Pakistan, where army-run residential areas are highly coveted, the DHA is one of the most expensive residential areas in Lahore. According to the presidential order by which it was formed, the DHA is an autonomous body with its own rules and regulations. In practice, however, it is not independent of the military; it is headed, in fact, by a serving army brigadier and the staff is largely made up of serving and retired army officers. The exact financial figures for Lahore DHA are not known but in Rawalpindi, close to the country's capital Islamabad, 3,375 acres of land was acquired for a Defence Housing Scheme (called MORGAH-I & II) at a cost of Rs.11 billion (US $189.65 million) and then sold for approximately Rs. 135 billion (US $2,328 million).[47] The DHA in Lahore, and those in other parts of the country, also sell its plots at an exorbitantly expensive price because it claims to be one of the best housing schemes in the city. In 2004, General Musharraf

defended these accumulated profits by claiming that the DHAs across
the country deserved the money they made because they provide services
that no other housing schemes can give.

> The defence *[sic]* societies everywhere are the top societies of Pakistan . . .
> why are we jealous if somebody gets a piece of land, cheap when it was
> initially *[sic]*, and because of the good work of the society, the prices rise
> by a hundred times and then the man earns some money.[48]

The Lahore DHA projects itself as offering its inhabitants, what it
calls, "modern living." The main office of the society is a large white-
washed building protected by high walls, edged with metal grills. Entry to
the building is carefully monitored, and one is only allowed in after
passing a series of metal detectors and security checkpoints. Once inside,
the vivid and bright interior stands in sharp contrast to the fortress-like
exterior. Large potted plants and exotic flowers are carefully placed in the
balconies and outside the windows. Colorful posters and large banners
decorate the walls advertising the latest plots and the new sectors that are
under development. One such poster, advertising the development of yet
another sector in the scheme, had the phrase "Modern Living" embel-
lished with a picture of a skyscraper and a shopping mall. The chief
administrator of the DHA also emphasized its modern aspects. In a personal interview, he mentioned that the scheme was so successful because
it provided an "alternate living concept for people."[49] He elaborated:

> You see . . . people everywhere, what is it that they really want in life?
> After working hard the whole day, they want to come back to a peaceful
> environment, to a clean, neat, and beautiful place. We in the DHA, we
> provide them with this. We have beautiful parks and recreational facili-
> ties, we have the best shopping plazas . . . all the top Western brands in
> Pakistan have a branch here. We provide people with all of this. We have
> the best roads, the best schools . . . everything that makes life comfort-
> able, we have it.

Later in the interview, we moved on to talk about ideas on modern life
and how the DHA tries to live up to peoples' expectations in this regard.

We discussed the posters that I had seen outside his office and what the DHA meant by "modern living." He explained,

> Over here [in DHA] we provide people with facilities and the means for a modern life. And what is modern? Well, to be modern is about being progressive, about moving ahead with the times . . . moving away from orthodox ideas and concepts. It is the ability to innovate. But, of course, this doesn't mean that we let go of our Muslim identity and our religion. This is our identity, our core, but it does not stop us from innovating, from moving with times and changing.

One cannot help be reminded, when hearing such remarks, of General Ayub Khan's description of progress and modernization, and its execution in the 1960s—the appeal to moving forward alongside an umbrella Muslim identity that would give Pakistan a unique identity on the "global stage." Echoing Ayub Khan's faith in "managing away" problems, the Brigadier believed that that the modern life of DHA was achieved and maintained through careful monitoring and imposition of order.

Unlike Doxiadis's Islamabad, that was developed following a single master plan, much of the DHA's development has been piecemeal, with new sectors added as the authority acquires more land. Most of this land, along the eastern periphery of Lahore, was agricultural and, given its proximity to India, had been left undeveloped for reasons of national security. As a result, it was largely unbuilt and the military used its influence to evacuate and move most of villages and settlements that existed in the area, but it had to build around the ones that it could not remove. However, as much as possible, the authority has emulated the rationalism of European modernist planning that had inspired Doxiadis in his own designs.

The gridiron pattern of the Defence Housing Authority in Lahore, with its emphasis on straight lines and geometric uniformity, lives up to Doxiadis's criteria of appropriate city planning. Such a layout in Lahore is, by no means, new. During General Ayub Khan's rule in the 1960s and under General Zia's in the 1980s, satellite towns and colonies were constructed along the city's southern periphery. Following the national trend in city planning these settlements were laid out in gridiron fashion. This was due partly to the prominence of modernist designs in the 1960s and partly for convenience: it was easier to lay down standard-issue sewage pipes and electric grids in straight lines and at right angles.[50] Unregulated growth has meant that most of these areas have changed considerably from their original layout but, in the DHA, all building plans and developments are carefully monitored to ensure their compliance to the layout. It is, according to the brigadier, the order of the place that is at the heart of its attractiveness for buyers.

At the same time, like the military government of the 1960s, the DHA builds its appeal through connections with the outside world and by drawing upon a wider sense of internationalism. This is visible in the presence of Western brands and restaurant chains, as the brigadier also emphasized, and, moreover, in also in the architectural style and tastes of the buildings constructed by the authority. In particular, the style of the mosques built by DHA are revealing of its broader frame of reference. During my meeting with the chief administrator, I learned that he took a keen interest in the design of the mosque and often helped in the design process.

> I have been all over the world . . . while in service, I was sent to Saudi Arabia, Syria, and Turkey. . . . I was most impressed by the buildings in Turkey. Now that I am here, I want people to see the beauty that I have seen. Islam has a wonderful and international heritage and we as Muslims should explore it.

The administrator's admiration of Turkey perhaps explains the presence in the Lahore DHA of a mosque resembling the Hagia Sophia. His comment about his travels also shows his sense of internationalism and his global frame of reference. Throughout our interview, the brigadier talked of famous mosques around the world. He was not concerned with how the mosques that he commissioned compared with other mosques in Pakistan; rather, he judged them by how they fit within an international frame of reference. Moreover, his sense of internationalism is grounded in the notion of a global community of Muslims and in a "generic Islam" that they all follow. On the one hand, the unanimity of "generic Islam" frames him within a larger Muslim identity that supersedes the national.

On the other hand, "generic Islam" conforms to prevailing sociopolitical norms and the modernist aspirations of the state and casts him as a modern individual. It is this sense of modern, one that is international but also compliant with local surroundings, that the brigadier wanted in the DHA, but could only attain through careful ordering.

It is not just the architecture of the mosques that reflects this broader vision of modern life, but also the proceedings within the mosque. Unlike mosques in other residential areas in Lahore, that are turned over to the neighborhood committee after construction or come under the jurisdiction of the *waqf* board, the mosques in Lahore's DHA (as in military cantonments) are entirely controlled by the central office. The mosques are maintained and overseen by the Religious Affairs Department of the central office. At the time of my fieldwork, the department was headed by a retired brigadier who, during service, had served as the director of religious instruction in the Education Corps. In his job at the DHA office, he was responsible for employing and overseeing all mosque staff—a *mu'azzin* to lead the call for prayers, a *khatīb* for Friday sermons, and a caretaker *(khādim)* for larger mosques. The selection process was left entirely to the brigadier, giving him considerable room for personal preferences. In our interview, however, he emphasized the "system and organization" of the selection. Reminiscent of Ayub Khan's reliance on order and efficiency in constructing a vision of modernity, the brigadier explained that the mosque staff were appointed through an "efficient system." An initial selection was based on qualifications, following which the candidates were called in for an interview and written test.

Order was also maintained through a strict monitoring of the content of Friday sermons in the mosques so as to not include any that went against "rational and educated thinking." Before the start of a new year, a list of topics is made and each *khatīb* is given a certain number of topics to prepare a sermon for. The prepared sermon needs to be based on the lecture given on that topic by the brigadier. Each *khatīb* has to submit his sermon to the brigadier who, after approving it, distributes copies of it among the staff. No *khatīb* was allowed to deviate from the distributed sermon. Unlike neighborhood mosques in other areas, where the *khatīb* is at liberty to express his views in the Friday sermons, the staff at DHA mosques are not allowed to speak on any topic that has not been approved.

The list of topics for 2009 revealed that the Friday sermons had three aims: to direct people away from popular rituals and customs, to make them aware of their religious duties and civic responsibilities, and to show the compatibility of religion with science. Individual topics ranged from "Should We Celebrate the Prophet's Birthday?" and the "True Concept of Sufism" to "Why Bribery Is Wrong" and "Why Gossip and Rumors Are Harmful." Science and technology was a regular theme as well, including topics such as "The Right Way of Using Technology" and "Islam and Science." The brigadier explained why he had chosen these topics:

> Over here [in DHA], we want to inculcate progressive values in people, something that is present in our religion. And we want to show them how to incorporate Islamic values and ideas in their daily life. This is what my aim is, that the sermons should help people live their lives as better Muslims.

The attention given to progressive values meant that the sermons inevitably contradicted customary practices inspired by Sufism—the sermon on not celebrating the Prophet's birthday being an obvious example. The brigadier, however, did not think that this was the case. During our interview, he insisted that what they were propagating in their mosques was not against Sufism or, for the matter, against any other sect. In particular, similar to the ideas on Sufism propagated under Ayub, he differentiated between the Sufis of the past who were pious men and the *pīrs* of today who manipulate the masses.

> The Sufis [in the past] were very religious and pious men, and they had a very strict code of ethics by which they lived their life. Even today, there are people who practice this kind of Sufism—for me, they are the real Sufis. These customary practices that we see today, they just take the name of Sufism, not its meaning or the way of life that it promotes.

The brigadier was keen to promote the values and ethics of "real" Sufis; their personal ethics, their tolerance and love for others and their devotion to Allah. According to him, these values "were worth promoting and common to all sects of Islam." In other words, he was appealing to "generic"

Islam, which steered clear of sectarian disputes while also propagating values that the DHA felt was compatible with its vision of modern life.

Much of what the DHA aspires to is reminiscent of Ayub's vision of modernism, but with one important difference. Here, rather than proclaiming it as a goal for the state, it is presented as a "lifestyle" for the people who live in DHA. Significantly, this is intended for all but reserved for those who, as the brigadier in charge of DHA said, have "made it." This kind of modern life, thus, has to be achieved through individual progress. The brigadier explained this as:

> Of course, nowadays there is a status element to living here. Not everyone can live here. Often, it is the culmination of a lifetime of hard work that one can build a house in the DHA. You work hard, you save, and then finally, one day you have a house here. Of course, it is about people wanting to show their success to the world, you want people to know that you have made it.

The modern image that the DHA tries to construct for itself is not always accepted, and it is not unusual to find people from all backgrounds who are critical of the DHA and the military more broadly. Equally, jokes about the military's aesthetics—particularly its penchant for straight lines—are also common. Architects who have worked with the military complain that its officers know neither Muslim history nor modern design. One architect, whose designs often reflect his interest in Islamic mysticism, explained why the military did not approve of his work: he had once submitted a plan for a mosque to be built at the Staff College in Quetta, and the generals in charge had immediately discarded it. His design was based on the idea of a paradise garden as reflected in the poetry of great mystics, such as the thirteenth-century Turkish Sufi Maulana Rumi. Apparently, one of the generals present had felt that the plan was sacrilegious as it aimed to create a second heaven on earth. "He told you that about innovation and change?" my architect informant scoffed.[51] "Army people, they are looking for straight lines, just like the parades they do and watch for years. That is all they know."

Another architect shared similar sentiments. He had once been asked to build a one-room house for a client on a piece of land in DHA. Since his client, a middle-aged teacher who lived alone, had asked for a large space with lots of light, the architect decided to build a structure that was completely round. The planning division of DHA, in charge of approving individual house plans, rejected this design immediately. The man in charge, a retired colonel, told the architect, "I find it very suspicious that you want to design a house like this. One room and that too in a circle. That's not a house."[52] The architect later suspected that since his client was a Zoroastrian, the colonel was paranoid and thought she had commissioned a temple. The architect said to me,

> That is what the generals [the army] are like. If it does not have four straight walls at straight angles and with four straight rooms, then it cannot be a house. There's modern for you. That piece of land [belonging to his client] had cost her millions and she could not even build a house there as she wanted.

Like the architects, many people belonging to established middle-class circles are also dismissive of the Lahore DHA. Spearheading the drive to revive the cultural and literary life of the city, they find that that the area lacks the "culture" and "tradition" of the Lahore that once was. The staunch sensibility of the military stands in sharp contrast to the religious attitudes of gentrified Lahoris, many of whom believe in some vague form of mysticism. Despite this, in the last decade, there has been an influx of people from these backgrounds to DHA.

Thus, we have seen in this chapter how the legacy of the "old" has been in dialogue with the "new" and the role of nostalgia in making this connection. In different ways, cultural, political, and military forces have synthesized old and new in the creation of the "modern" in Pakistan. The international frame—Pakistan's position within the larger world—and the role of an imagined outsider has been critical to this process.

TWO

Moral Rhetoric,
Modernity, and Class

STANDING NEAR a busy intersection of Canal Road, the artery that connects the older parts of the city with the new, it is hard to imagine a Lahore of Ava Gardner, jazz evenings, and old-world charms. At all times of the day, the four-lane road is littered with cars, buses, motorcycles, and rickshaws, leaving the air thick with fumes. On most days, especially in the winter months, a yellow-brown haze of dust, exhaust fumes, and pollution colors the atmosphere. This was once charmingly described by a historian as giving Lahore a "sepia-color" tinge, but it is brutal to breathe on a regular basis.[1] Population growth has not been matched by the expansion of public transport. Instead, every half decade, the main roads of the city are expanded by an additional lane, a process that often involves cutting down the trees that lined them and reducing the size of the surrounding sidewalks. Even after such actions, during rush hours, one can remain stranded in traffic for hours and, save for those who can afford air-conditioning in their cars, with little respite from the blistering sun. In such instances, many people turn off their car engines, others step outside for a cigarette break and some angrily honk their car horns. In recent years, the city has also faced the brunt of the country's power shortage; in summer months, when the thermometer can rise up to 50 degrees Celsius (122 degrees Fahrenheit) scheduled power cuts, or "load shedding" as it is called, total sixteen to twenty hours per day. Looking at the dust-ridden market buildings near the canal, amid the noise, one cannot help but be reminded of the hollowness of the modern(ist) promise and pleasures of cities, big roads, and fast cars.

Despite the difference between the city that was promised and what exists now, or perhaps because of it, the modernist dream continues to prevail. It exists, as the last chapter demonstrated, in the nostalgia that is felt for the Lahore of the past, and in the efforts to revive the social and public culture of that time. In this chapter, I unravel its presence in class contestations and moral rhetoric in middle-class Lahore. Specifically, I examine the ways in which nostalgia for and association with the Lahore of yesteryears—the lost modern—becomes a form of distinction; it is a way for the older inhabitants of the city to distinguish themselves from the new. To do so, I first shed light on the different groups that constitute the middle class in Lahore, followed by a discussion of the different rhetorical strategies that are deployed. In particular, I focus on rhetoric surrounding modernism and authenticity, and discourses on moral life and Islam.

THE MIDDLE-CLASS MILIEU

As is generally the case with literature on Pakistan, Lahore is often seen as missing a middle-class population. Within Pakistan, Lahore is stereo-typically described as a big village where everyone knows everyone else. Such sentiments imply that Lahore has a rural or provincial feel, despite its size and status as the cultural capital of the country. For instance, con-sider this lighthearted memoir of a Karachite's time in Lahore:

> Today, any red-blooded Karachi-walla will tell you that Lahoris are "paindus" *[paindō]* (village idiots) with no sense of class, culture or manners. Similarly, any red-blooded Lahori will tell you that Karachites are social upstarts with no sense of class, cultures or manners....
>
>   . . . Karachites pride themselves for being sophisticated, modern and forward-looking whereas Lahoris, they believe, are content to live on

the laurels of the past and spend their days eating copious amounts of food and ogling women (in fact they expend so much energy in ogling women that they have to eat such large quantities of food merely to maintain their strength). Lahoris, on the other hand, see themselves as the standard-bearers of gracious tradition and old-world hospitality.[2]

Karachites often moan that not only does everyone in Lahore know everyone else, but everyone also knows what the other is doing and there is no privacy. People in Lahore, it is argued, have no individual identity and are only known by their surnames and family ties.

The perception that Lahore is a big village is rooted in the demographic changes that took place during Partition, as well as, I would suggest, in the trends toward upward mobility that were established in the subsequent decades. Pre-Partition Lahore was a thriving urban and commercial center comprising Muslim, Hindu, Sikh, Christian, and some Parsi families. As in other parts of colonial India, the urban population of Lahore was largely dependent on the state. It consisted of groups that were beneficiaries of government employment and education, as well as those who were involved more indirectly with the colonial public sphere, such as traders and businessmen.[3] The top layer of the indigenous urban population consisted of gazetted government officials, lawyers, and prosperous traders and businessmen. People falling into this group were what is classically considered the colonial middle class. Though educated in state schools and imbibing the modernist values of its corresponding class in Britain, however, they were not of middling rank in terms of their economic and social position within India. Many of them were very wealthy—in particular, the majority of Muslim and Sikh families that came from landed backgrounds—and were considered part of the local elite rather than middle class. In terms of station, "middle class" more adequately described aspiring groups further down the socioeconomic ladder. They too were predominantly reliant on the state, and were employed as clerical and municipal-level government officials, teachers, and small businessmen and traders. Many of these families belonged to the walled city of Lahore, and had moved from there to newer areas after finding government employment. Others were migrants to Lahore, often with connections to *mufassalite* traders.[4]

There were no strict rules governing occupation, but commercial activities—shops, small and large businesses, trading, and money lending—were largely confined to the city's Hindu and Parsi residents.[5] The Muslim and Sikh families predominantly came from agricultural backgrounds and maintained connections to land. In particular, Muslims who were part of the city's elite belonged to families that had sided with the British during the annexation of Punjab in 1849 and, in return, were rewarded with agricultural land and jobs in the colonial government. During Partition in 1947, Lahore lost its ethnic and religious diversity when most of the Hindu and Sikh populations crossed the newly created border and left for India.[6] Some of the Parsi and Christian population remained in Lahore at the time of Partition but started leaving in subsequent years. The mass exodus of Hindus at the time of Partition also left a hole in the commercial sector of Lahore that was not filled by the incoming population. Many of those who arrived in Lahore from across the border came from the agricultural lands of what is now East Punjab and either remained involved in farming or joined the civil service in the new country. There was, thus, an overwhelming presence of groups from agricultural backgrounds. Moreover, many of the affluent landowning families (who comprised the top strata of Lahore) had been educated in the same schools. This meant that such groups tended to know each other—giving the city the rural-like feel that certain Karachites so despise.

In addition, I argue that the trend toward upward mobility which developed in the early decades after Partition also contributed to the sense that Lahore had no middle class. Although the incoming migrants came predominantly from agricultural or *ashraf* backgrounds, many of them became involved in professional occupations. Those who were more affluent and had previously served as gazetted government officials in the colonial state were given senior positions within the bureaucracy. These groups were accommodated within elite residential areas such as Model Town or the Civil Station. Others who were less affluent settled into the middle-class professions of teaching, journalism, law, and medicine or were employed within government institutions. As I discussed in Chapter 1, such families were often settled in the low-cost housing schemes of Samanabad, or in nearby residential areas such as Ichra. They were joined here by other aspiring professionals, many of whom had migrated to Lahore from small towns or had originally lived in the walled city. Together, these groups comprised the middle class, but they were small in number and the boundary between them, on the one hand, and the urban elite, on the other, was not always clear. As I described earlier, many of them had family and kin connections with those in more senior positions in the bureaucracy. Moreover, government subsidies and support—made available in 1950s and 1960s—allowed middle-class families to send their children to elite institutions. There was, thus, some intermingling of the two groups. Much of this was, of course, made possible because of the reduced size of the city following Partition and a scaled-back urban public sphere. Although class distinctions remained and not all families interacted with each other, the small public sphere allowed people, as discussed in Herbert Gans *Urban Villagers* (1962), to know of each other. In later years, when many of these middle-class families prospered and moved to elite residential areas, the boundary between the two groups became even more blurred. This led to the general perception that Lahore predominantly consists of two groups of people: an urban elite, often with landed connections, and a working-class population of small traders or artisans who lived and worked in the old walled city. According to such depictions, a middle stratum is absent.

However, following the national pattern of urbanization, the demography of Lahore has changed drastically since Partition, particularly in the last three decades. Between 1951 and 1980, the population of Lahore grew from 849,333 to 2,952,698. In the 1998 national census, the city's population had increased to 6.5 million.[7] By 2001, the Lahore Metropolitan Corporation estimated that 7.7 million people lived in Lahore, and although at the time of this writing the 2017 census has not been completed, urban planners and nongovernmental organizations operating in the city estimate Lahore's population to be more than 9 million.[8] This expansion has predominantly involved population growth as well as the arrival of different groups from other parts of Punjab.

In my reading, two points need to be made here. First, the city has been a site of significant rural-to-urban migration. In the 1960s, when Punjab's agricultural production was bolstered by Ayub Khan, many mid-level farmers prospered enough to move with their families to Lahore while maintaining ties to their lands. Small farmers, who were squeezed out due to the green revolution, also moved to Lahore to look for alternative work. Increased economic activity and industrial production at the time also acted as a pull factor. Even after the 1960s, rural migrants continued to move to Lahore, attracted by employment and educational prospects in the city. By the mid-1970s to the 1980s, when labor migration to the Persian Gulf states was at its peak, remittances sent home by relatives allowed many rural families to move to the city.[9] Coming mainly from small towns and villages in Punjab, this group consists of small businessmen, traders, teachers, and low- to mid-level government officials as well as engineers, lawyers, and doctors. Increasingly, many of them are employed within the city's expanding private sector, working as mid-level employees in local and multinational banks and other corporations.

Second, Lahore has also been a site for what can loosely be described as urban-to-urban migration by a number of different groups. The arrival of groups from small towns and villages has been complemented by the in-migration of families associated with the industrial towns of Faisalabad and Chiniot. As owners of sugar and flour mills in Chiniot, and textile mills in Faisalabad, such families have significant wealth and often maintain residences in both Lahore and their native towns. In Lahore, the residence serves as a base for accessing education in elite private schools for their children, as well as a way to enjoy the recreational life of a big city. Lahore has also been a site for migration from other Pakistani cities. In the 1990s, a large number of people, disturbed by the political and ethnic violence in Karachi, moved to Lahore. Similarly, following ethnic tensions and separatist movements in Balochistan, many Punjab families that had been settled in Quetta for decades moved back to Lahore.

In the last two decades, Lahore has been the site for return-migration by both highly skilled professionals and semi-skilled groups from the United States and, to a lesser extent, Britain and the Gulf. A brief explanation of Pakistani migration patterns can be useful here. In broad terms, there have been two distinct forms of migration to the United States. First, beginning in the 1960s and continuing to the present, one has seen a steady flow of educated and skilled professionals from Pakistan to the United States. This group predominantly consists of doctors and engineers, but also includes businesspersons and students who initially went to pursue tertiary education abroad before settling. Such migrants come from a variety of backgrounds. Some of them belong to affluent families, went to pursue undergraduate and graduate degrees in the United States, and have since advanced into professions such as law, finance, and consultancy work. Others do not come from well-established backgrounds, but were able to study in state-subsidized medical colleges and engineering universities in Pakistan. These individuals subsequently used their education to emigrate to the United States for work or further education. Second, starting in the 1980s, there has been a flow of workers from Pakistan who adopt jobs such as taxi driving, restaurant work, and construction employment.[10]

Since the mid-1990s, a return-migration is under way on the part of both groups. Attracted by the relatively stable political environment of the time, many highly skilled migrants decided to return. Others did not move back permanently, but bought property in the city to use when they came back for holidays or, more commonly, to rent. Although no statistical data has been collected on such forms of migration, most real-estate agents and developers in Lahore agree that the boom in the city's property market is due to investment of foreign capital. Lahore is not the only case. Chak Shahzad, a suburb of Islamabad that is known for its luxurious farmhouses and large estates, is mainly occupied by expats who have returned from the United States and still maintain their foreign links. Similarly, many semi-skilled migrants have also returned, using their experience and money to start small businesses or to invest in property. The return of these migrants, particularly in the case of highly skilled migrants, has often been represented in mainstream media as a consequence of the problems of growing Islamophobia and racial discrimination in the United States, particularly following the Gulf Wars and 9/11 attacks. In my experience, however, while many return-migrants spoke of these problems, in most cases their return home was motivated primarily by the need to look after, or to be close to, elderly parents and family members. Following the financial crisis and slowdown of the U.S. economy, the loss of jobs has also motivated return-migration within both groups.

The influx of people from smaller towns in Punjab has been paralleled by population growth and the advancement of groups indigenous to the city. In the walled city, economic and social advancement has corresponded with a shift to newer parts of town.[11] This shift overlaps with the colonial rule pattern noted by Daechsel, where prosperous families from the walled city started to move to new middle-class residential areas, but with some significant differences.[12] In Daechsel's analysis, it was government employment that prompted families to move away from the walled city into the middle-class life of colonial Lahore. The more recent shifts of the last three to four decades have not involved government employment but growth in the business and commercial sector. There has been considerable upward mobility among businessmen and traders operating within the largely informal economy of wholesale trade in food and cloth. As these groups have prospered, they have expanded their business ventures into the formal economy outside of the walled city. For instance, many of them own, or have close ties to, department stores and shops in affluent parts of city. The rise in income levels of this group has been complemented with increased education; while many of the traders operating in the 1980s may not have received formal education, their children are likely to have attended school and college. In many cases, their children have completed business and marketing degrees and have used such skills to further expand into the formal sector. Most of these prosperous business families have now moved away from the walled city, often to newer residential areas in the southwest or northern periphery, but sometimes also to the neighborhoods of Gulberg and Garden Town. This move, however, has not resulted in a complete break from life in the walled city, as Daechsel notes in his analysis, because many continue to hold commercial interests in the area.

MODERNISM AND AUTHENTICITY

For the rest of the chapter, I want to focus on the rhetorical strategies at play within this wider middle-class milieu. In this first instance, I explore how, in Lahore and urban Pakistan more broadly, moral debate and class contestation often deploy discourses on modernity and tradition. This was first noted by Richard Murphy in his ethnographic account of class rhetoric in Lahore, a study based on fieldwork conducted in the early 1990s when the middling strata was not as expansive as it would later become. Here, I discuss some of his insights and then refine them in relation to the demographic changes visible in my ethnography. Murphy argued that moral debate in Lahore often oscillated between competing claims of modernism and authenticity.[13] The modernist perspective, based on a global discourse of economic development and progress, saw Lahore and, in fact, the rest of the country as "underdeveloped" or "backward." Education, industrial growth, and technological advances were seen as a way toward, and also a sign of, progress. Within this classic postcolonial depiction, connections to the outside world—articulated through fluency in English and knowledge of Western architecture and culture, travel, and consumption of luxury goods—were seen as signs of modernity and, consequently, of status and prestige. At a broader level, "representation of literacy and education often conflated with class."[14] Claims to education and refinement were a way for established urban groups to put down the upwardly mobile; wealth and economic ascent did not always lead to a change in social status because such families were still considered illiterate and therefore "backward." Implicit in these ways of thinking was not only a "concept of time lived forward in moral and chronological terms" but also the old Enlightenment idea that man is a rational animal. Murphy writes here that

> just as nineteenth-century British administrators justified their rule on the grounds they had come to civilize a "backward" subcontinent, modern urban Pakistanis justify the moral subordination of . . . poor people and nouveau riche by figuring them as irrational, hence less than fully human beings.[15]

Murphy found that, conversely, the desire for progress existed alongside a discourse of authenticity where the past was romanticized. Among the established and, often, Westernized Lahoris, connections to the past were sutured through genealogy and family association along with an appreciation of antiques, "ethnic" clothing and interior design, and historic buildings. These perspectives were not mutually exclusive, and Lahoris often shifted from one to another, sometimes in the same argument. They were part of the rhetorical strategies through which class hierarchies were negotiated and established.[16] Both strategies—using education to assert refinement and establishing links to the past—coalesced around the category of *khāndānī* (lit. "of family"). Individuals who were of old-money background or possessed genealogical ties to distinguished families and notables of the past were marked as *khāndānī*. Although Murphy does not mention this, my own ethnography indicates that the notables with whom *khāndānī* families usually claim links were from *ashraf* backgrounds, or had served as high-ranking government officials in colonial India and were, in some cases, associated with the nationalist movement. Such ties, as I argue below, allow them to ground themselves not only within the past but also with the broader history of progressivism in the subcontinent. This was certainly the case with what Murphy referred to as "Lahore Society"—*khāndānī* families who formed the elite set of the city. He writes that such families equated education with social refinement and status; the political elite and civil servants belonging to "Lahore Society" often cited lack of education and "backwardness" as the root cause of the country's many economic and political problems.[17] At the same time, they distinguished themselves from other educated and wealthy families through their personal histories and association with past notables of the city.

The rhetorical strategies that Murphy described remain valid today. However, although the notion remains central to negotiating and establishing class hierarchies, the arrival of new groups and the expansion of existing groups—described previously—often make it difficult to establish who exactly is *khāndānī*. Many of the old-money families have married into new money, while some have left Pakistan to settle abroad but return frequently. Neither is it clear how deep an association one needs to develop to be accepted as *khāndānī*. Similar to the ambiguity noted by Salamandra in the category *ibn 'a'ileh* (urban notable) in Damascus, *khāndānī*, in practice, is used for families with well-known historical connections as well as those who may not have any notable pedigree.[18] In Lahore, the status is claimed by old-money families who composed the elite of the post-Partition urban public sphere, as well as the middle-class groups of the time who prospered largely through government and public employment. In addition, *khāndānī* is often adopted by expat families, particularly those employed in the medical profession, many of whom do not possess links to the city's history, but are affluent, well-educated, and familiar with Western culture and mannerisms.

Equally, wealth and status derived from success in the industrial and corporate sector are a source of tension. Prominent civil servants, many of whom are retired, and those associated with the state-employed middle class of the 1960s often lament that _khāndānī_ families acquired their reputation from their work and not from the money they possessed. As the spouse of a retired diplomat commented, "In our time, people got status from their [government] service, for what they did for people and the country. These days, it is only about money. Even businessmen are considered _khāndānī_."[19] In turn, prominent families with business and private sector interests claim that they help create jobs in the country, while the high-ranking government officials are just interested in ruling over people. However, these two spheres also often overlap, not least because of intermarriages between the two groups. More significantly, the offspring of prominent civil servants and members of the old middle class have also branched into the private sector. The shift toward the private sector has been read by Arif Hasan as part of a larger process of "elite alienation" in Pakistan.[20] He argues that the nationalization policies introduced by Zulfiqar Ali Bhutto in the 1970s and, more importantly, the Islamization agenda of Zia in the 1980s resulted in the retreat of the (largely secular) established urban groups from the public domain. Although I mostly agree with Hasan's analysis, I would also suggest that this retreat needs to considered within the context of the democratization of the government sector and the resulting loss of the monopoly over bureaucratic power. This was certainly visible in the moral rhetoric that produces hierarchies based on discourses of progress. While government service by the older generation in a family gave it a claim of being _khāndānī_, present-day linkages with the government are often considered a sign of corruption, symptomatic of the "backwardness" of those who now dominate the public sphere.

Although family names and histories remain central to moral debate, it is often the social disposition—what Bourdieu has termed "habitus"—that confirms an individual's position as _khāndānī_.[21] Class position, in this context, is determined by an acquired set of tastes, sensibilities, and orientation toward the wider world. This particular habitus is manifested through a careful balance between discourses of modernism and authenticity. In present-day Lahore, this form of distinction is often expressed, as discussed in Chapter 1, through participation in literary and artistic endeavors and by a broader identification with the kind of nostalgia for an idealized middle-class life. Gentrified and affluent Lahoris often arrange and attend artistic and literary events aimed at reviving the cultural life of their city. Similarly, many possess a deference for Sufi poetry and classical *gazal*, and regularly attend concerts and musical evenings, often held in old houses in the walled city. This taste for the "authentic" attaches them to the general history of the region and to the broader history of Muslim culture. At the same time, participating in such activities also provides linkages to a specific history of progressivism as it is imagined in the contemporary discourse surrounding the "lost modern" in Lahore. Possessing familiarity with that world, through genealogies and family associations, as well as mannerisms and tastes, becomes a way of asserting oneself as part of the established *khāndānī* classes of Lahore and, by contrast, to differentiate oneself from newer urban groups.

Class rhetoric and forms of distinction within this register often rely upon an ideal of modern life that is similar in many respects to the model that was propagated during Ayub Khan's rule. In the 1950s and 1960s, the ideal urban citizen was constructed as one who was educated, and therefore progressive and rational, while ensconced in Urdu literary culture and styles of comportment. Within contemporary moral and class rhetoric in Lahore, the emphasis is not so much on Urdu literary culture alone, but rather on a more general appreciation of culture and literary traditions. Certainly, knowledge of Urdu writers and poets continues to be considered as a sign of refinement, but it now also extends to an appreciation of Sufi poetry and songs, many of which are in Punjabi, as well as local folk traditions. However, the broader ideal of being knowledgeable and cultured in particular art forms, while still inhabiting progressive and rational attitudes, is similar to the ideas promoted by Ayub Khan. Moreover, this form of distinction often makes use of writings, poetry, and aesthetics informed by left-wing activism from the 1950s but, in the process, transforms them from a specific critique of the establishment to a general symbol of the progressivism of the time. For instance, concerts celebrating the poetry of Faiz Ahmad Faiz are well-attended by gentrified Lahoris. For many such people, the poetry is emblematic of a progressive middle-class ethos that they believe is now lost. The middle-class culture that is mourned and remembered at such events is devoid of the politics that existed at the time; the lack of consensus on national culture, the tensions between different ideological and ethnic groups, and the shifting stance on the place of religion in urban life are all blurred out of memory. Instead, against a backdrop of visible religiosity in the public sphere and the ever-present specter of religious violence, it is remembered for its overall commitment to progressivism—ideals that gentrified Lahoris associate with themselves but, from their perspective, are neither valued by the conservative upwardly mobile and new urban groups, nor propagated by the state.

In such a setting, not only do these rhetorical strategies and forms of distinction establish who is and who is not *khāndānī* but, moreover, the category itself is produced through such contestations. Among affluent groups of similar socioeconomic status, such contestation takes on the form of agonistic competition, with members of each group asserting themselves through their strongest attributes. Those who have the right genealogy claim that it is, ultimately, descent that distinguishes *khāndānī* families from others. Meanwhile, members of the old middle-class contend that living on the laurels of one's ancestors alone is not enough, and that one is *khāndānī* through one's values and way of living. In a discussion of well-known families of Lahore, a retired lecturer from a government institution remarked that not all of them were *khāndānī*. Mentioning a landed family known for their connections with the British in colonial Punjab, she commented, "There is a difference between *khāndānī* and *ujaṛe nāwāb*."[22] Similarly, families involved in professional work or with a history of government service may be dismissive of those involved in commercial and business initiatives, yet it is the latter who support many literary and artistic endeavors in Lahore. Expat families who move in the same circles as established Lahoris assert their position through a broader appeal to cosmopolitanism and progressive lifestyles. Although there are cleavages and competition between these groups, there is also considerable intermingling, often through marriage, friendships, and family associations.

The contested nature of the category gives it considerable flexibility, making it open for new groups and families to enter *khāndānī* circles through a careful utilization of the social and economic capital available to them. Yet it remains closed to those who do not possess the required attributes or the skills to maneuver through them. While more affluent families, part of the upper echelons of the expanded middle strata of Lahore, may over time acquire the requisite capital and dispositions to enter such contestations, those who fall in the middling or lower ranks often possess neither the attributes nor, in some cases, the inclination. Moreover, contestations for *khāndānī* status involve not only distinguishing oneself from those of the same rank, but also differentiating between those who are above and below. In the context where social hierarchies are centered around the idea of progress, conceived as a move forward in both the moral and chronological senses, groups lower down the socioeconomic ladder are often depicted as "backward." In everyday class rhetoric, urban groups that are not considered part of established circles are often referred to as *shahri* or *bāzārī*. *Shahri* literally means "town dweller," whereas *bāzārī* translates as "of the bazaar"; both terms imply vulgarity and notoriety and usually suggest questionable personal morals. The term *paindō*—which means "village idiot"—is also commonly used but, like *shahri* and *bāzārī*, more generally denotes uncultured tastes and, more importantly, an uncultivated mind.

At the same time, just as *khāndānī* status depend on linkages to the progressive past of the region, new urban groups, particularly those of middling and lower ranks, were often associated with the "regressive" era in Pakistan's history. In this respect, they are often depicted as heavily influenced by Zia's Islamization policies. Visible signs of religiosity within these groups—for instance, wearing a beard or veiling—is often viewed as an example of the growing presence of Wahhabism. Many people in *khāndānī* circles would often complain that the middle class is filled with people holding extremist views on religion and that many of them are sympathetic toward the Taliban and other militant groups. Although the "middle class" is an all-encompassing term, used for and by all urban groups except the poor, most established groups self-identify as upper middle class. This latter category is deployed, in such instances, derogatorily for new urban groups. Such depictions of new urban groups were particularly common in 2010—the year that the majority of the fieldwork for this book was conducted—when Lahore had experienced several suicide attacks by the Pakistani Taliban. In this tense environment, established groups in the city would explain the violence—both to themselves and to an outside audience—as a legacy of Zia's promotion of jihad. Here, they would complain that the mind-set of the new middle class was part of the problem of religious extremism, claiming that many such groups identified with, and glorified the idea of, jihad. After a suicide blast in a large market in Lahore on the night before Eid, an attack which left sixty-one people dead, much of the conversation in established circles, and in the English-language newspapers favored by them, revolved around the lack of condemnation of the Taliban in the wider population. As one senior journalist remarked, "The trouble is that our middle class are all Taliban apologists because they still see them as fighting a glorious jihad."[23]

Aware of these stereotypes, members of the new middle class would challenge these depictions by pointing out that it was them, rather than the established groups, who were the real victims of the religious violence in the country. In a conversation in the week following the attack on the market, a schoolteacher in a primary school, who lived in the area, remarked to me, "All the *amīr log* [rich people] blame ordinary people for supporting Taliban, but tell me, who is it that suffers when there is a bomb attack . . . has there ever been an attack in a place where rich people go? It's the middle class that is dying, not them."[24] The schoolteacher's comments were informed by a broader critique, within upwardly mobile and middle-class circles, of the privileged and secluded lifestyles of affluent Lahoris. Taunting them for such declared lack of awareness of the city, they claimed that affluent Lahoris have enough money and connections that they do not need to deal with the daily grit and grind of city life. As an informant once put it, "What do they [gentrified Lahoris] know about Lahore; they spend their days in gymkhanas and clubs, never need to step out into the real world because everything is delivered to their doorsteps."[25] The younger generation, in particular, were referred to as "burgers," indicating Westernized lifestyles and a general unfamiliarity with local ways and norms.

In such moments of criticism, upwardly mobile groups often present themselves as the real "sons of the soil"—much like the *ibn al-balād* of Cairo—while affluent Lahoris, by contrast, are cast away into their secluded elite circles.[26] In such discourses, their portrayal reflects the broader retreat of the old middle class and, affluent Lahoris more generally, to the private sphere. While linkages to the government were central to middle-class identity in the 1950s and 1960s, the younger generation of old middle-class families rarely study in public institutions and are predominantly employed in the private sector. It is this absence that allows the upwardly mobile families—a majority of whom are educated in government institutions—to think of the offspring of established Lahoris as "burger" and as alienated from everyday life in the city. The older generation of old middle-class families often agree with this, lamenting that their children do not know how to survive in the city. However, this often becomes a way of reasserting their own moral authority and superiority. Since the public sphere—and the urban groups that now dominate it—are conceived as corrupt and backward, the inability of their children to survive in such spaces becomes a way of highlighting their own progressive values.

Just as the old middle class claims moral superiority over others through its progressive values, new middle-class groups assert their position by pointing toward the lack of morality within the socioeconomic groups above them. They argue that the upper class may have wealth at their disposal, but it came at a cost of morality and meaning in their lives. These claims are often made through reflections on what it means to lead a moral Muslim life, discussions which the next section addresses.

MORAL LIFE AND ISLAM

Parallel to discourses on modernism and authenticity, moral debate in Lahore often centers on the notion of a good Muslim and on what it means to lead a meaningful moral life. In such discussions, Lahoris often evoke the notion of *asl*, literally meaning "authentic" or "real." The inability to locate, recognize, and follow *asl* Islam is used both as an explanation of, and as a form of critique for, the current state of affairs in Pakistan, as well as the Muslim world more broadly. Thus, when conversing in this register, most people contend that the main problem with the contemporary Islamic world is that people are Muslim only in name, but not in their actions and pursuits. They maintain that if Muslims would understand and pursue "real" Islam, then they would be able to solve the problems in which they are currently engulfed. For instance, many Lahoris claim that that if Pakistanis were "real" Muslims, the country would be rid of the

problems of corruption, economic and social underdevelopment, and terrorism. The idea that the key to individual and collective success lies in
correct religious practices and values reflects, what Francis Robinson
termed, the turn toward this-worldly Islam in nineteenth-century
reformist movements in South Asia.[27] Moreover, such ways of thinking
reflect the "generic" Islam of the state, mentioned earlier, that not only
uses religion to construct an umbrella identity for the nation but also
functionalizes it. However, while the sense that *asl* Islam can be, as Starrett
describes it, "put to work" draws from this-worldly reform traditions and
"generic" state Islam, the wider discourse around it incorporates and uti-
lizes ideas that far extend these sources.[28] As is generally the case, an
appeal to the authentic denotes the presence and the desire to return to
the original but, as I illustrate, also allows space for considerable innovation and experimentation.[29]

In everyday moral rhetoric during my fieldwork, *asl* Islam was invariably defined in relation to what it was not. It was commonly used as a
form of criticism. For instance, while mentioning that most Lahoris did
not pray regularly, an informant commented that *asl* Muslims were those
who did not need to be reminded of their duties and had incorporated
daily prayers in their routine. Conversely, a manager at a local bank often
complained that his employees took too many breaks for prayers: "This is
not Islam—always taking off from work. In essence, real Islam is about
the commitment with which you attend to all your duties, not just
praying."[30] Similarly, after a visit to his daughter in the United States, a
retired doctor told me that he was very impressed with the work ethic of
the people he saw: "They may not identify as Muslims, but with the fair-
ness and discipline with which they live and treat others, they are following the real Islam."[31] In relation to growing religious intolerance,
many people would often argue that *asl* Islam lay in humanism that was
preached by Sufis like Bulleh Shah. Such rhetoric was not confined to
those who self-identified as religious, but was used by people of all kinds
of religious sensibilities and political leanings. For instance, in reference
to the growing trend of veiling in Pakistan, many liberals maintained that
asl Islam was about modesty and respectful behavior among both men
and women, and it was unnecessary to veil. Similarly, when a friend was
labeled as an atheist *(lādīn)* by a religious party's student union for his

communist beliefs, he retorted *asl* Islam was about economic redistribution and equality. Commenting on the appearance of the student union
members, he said, "There is more to Islam than growing a beard." These
different positions on *asl* Islam were by no means mutually exclusive.
Depending on the context—the position of the speaker and audience at
hand—most people shifted from one position to another, sometimes even
within the same conversation.

Much like the discourse on modernism and authenticity, an appeal to
asl Islam was often a moral claim, a way of establishing one's position in
relation to others.[32] It was thus a way to critique the privileged position of
those higher up in the larger social hierarchy. Returning from a frustrating
day at the local courts, a schoolteacher complained that he had spent the
whole day waiting for his turn, but he was never called to present his
documents to the judge. Instead, the judge kept entertaining cases of
people who did not have an appointment for the day, but were previously
known to him or his colleagues. "It was all about who had paid whom and
who knew whom," he said. "And then," the teacher continued, "he [the
judge] had the nerve to take a prayer break. Doesn't bother to know what
the Quran says about dishonesty but wants to show the world he is
a Muslim by praying. That is not Islam." Such moral rhetoric is quite
common in Lahore, and serves as a way to condemn the behavior of
others while also establishing the credentials of the speaker. The judge
may have enjoyed a more prestigious and influential position but, through
his appeal to the Quran—the *asl* Islam, in this context—the schoolteacher
was able to assert himself as morally superior. As mentioned earlier, such
rhetorical strategies were not limited to those who considered themselves
as pious or, as in this case, well-versed in the Quran. Like many Pakistanis
the schoolteacher had learned to read the Quran in Arabic when he was
a teenager, but without any commentary or translation. In more recent
years, he had read the translations and commentary of some chapters and
often expressed the desire to study all of it one day when he had more
time. His criticism of the judge was based on his more general knowledge
of the topics covered in the Quran. Moreover, it was an indication of his
broader belief that *asl* Islam should not be about following religious
prescription without any regard for other obligations and duties.

Such rhetoric illustrates how, despite the normativity of Islam, religious discourses operate within a broader economy of knowledge.[33] Not only were a range of moral concerns discussed through Islam but, moreover, the religious ideals that were drawn upon were often legitimized in relation to existing needs and anxieties. Echoing the wider perception, within Pakistan and outside, Lahoris of all backgrounds often complained that within the current climate of religious violence the space for debate and deliberation on Islam was disappearing. Yet, such complaints and condemnations were evidence in themselves of the prevailing room for debate. Groups and organizations that were held responsible for the shrinking space for dialogue, such as the Taliban, were frequently discussed and criticized for misinterpreting what *asl* Islam was. While it was true that there existed a general fear and reluctance to openly voice opinions, everyday conversations reflected an active engagement with ideas on Islam and its place in individual and public life. In such contexts, Islamic discourses were deployed not simply to make a moral point, but as part of a broader display of intellectual dexterity and knowledge about the world.

I am, of course, aware here that as much as discussions evoking *asl* Islam displayed a sense of liveliness and creativity that runs contrary to popular perceptions of Islamic revivalism, they were nevertheless colored by the presence of the latter. Anthropological work on Islamic reformism in South Asia rightly reminds us that contemporary movements, much like their nineteenth-century counterparts, are discursively constructed and open to considerable change.[34] Moreover, as Humeira Iqtidar has demonstrated in the case of Lahore, the engagement of Islamism with the political domain, as well as the competition between Islamist groups, can stimulate a broader rationalization of religious practice.[35] However, we need to remember that while the Islamic revival may provoke deliberation, it also often sets the limit of the debate, not just for itself but also for its opposition. In such a context, the recourse to *asl* Islam for critique is not just an example of the democratization of religious interpretation, made possible by mass education and fragmented authority. It is also evidence that many of my informants felt that this was the only space left for opposition.

At a broader level, the moral rhetoric described here captures not only the openness and aspirational quality of Islam in Pakistan, noted by

Naveeda Khan, but also the skepticism that comes with it.[36] Drawing upon Bergson's notion of time, as understood by the poet and philosopher Muhammad Iqbal, Khan argues that aspirational striving in Pakistan opens up room for experimentation, while the fear of ossification leads to skepticism of everyday religious life. This was certainly noticeable in the rhetoric around *asl* Islam which was invariably presented as missing from the present and having to be discovered. The need to reflect upon what it means to be a Muslim represents a desire to move toward a higher under-standing, to be, as Khan has termed it, in a constant state of becoming. At the same time, the skepticism, and criticism, of people who are perceived as only following standard religious practice points toward the broader fear of ossification, that is, a sense of coming to a standstill. Khan situates this aspirational quality of Islam in the creation of Pakistan—the con-struction of a space that allows for Muslim striving.[37] While Khan is able to draw out the multiple possibilities and futures that arise from this aspirational quality, she rarely considers other forms of striving and aspirations—both at the individual and collective levels—and how they may have influenced those debated projects of becoming.

In particular, aspirations for progress are deeply entangled with concep-tions of Muslim nationalism and the creation of Pakistan. Not only was the quest for progress—a promise to bring modernity home—a key concern for the Muslim League in the lead up to independence, but it remained an enduring theme in subsequent decades.[38] As described in the last chapter, it was this desire for advancement that shaped a particular vision of moder-nity and modern life which continues to hold immense sway in today's Pakistan. Questions of modernity and progress—the decline of Muslim power and the sense of marginality and of being "under siege"—were the impetus for and the subject of nineteenth-century Islamic reform move-ments. In this respect, the aspirational quality of Islam emerging from Muslim nationalism, and experimentation that it makes space for, cannot be separated from broader desires for progress and advancement. [39] Such linkages have continued to evolve and strengthen in national discourse, particularly through the functionalization of religion by the Pakistani state. Moreover, at the local level, these connections are visible in class politics in Lahore, where moral and social hierarchies are constructed in relation to discourses of progress and modernity.

As we have seen in the rhetoric surrounding *asl* Islam, the moral ideal that is evoked is closely associated with a broader aspiration for both individual and collective progress. Moreover, it highlights how ideas on *asl* Islam are inherently relational. They are dependent on not just the social context but also the moral space that a person occupies. In other words, they are often understood and constructed in opposition to those considered above or below in the wider hierarchy. In the following section, I explore how this moral and social hierarchy and, in particular, one's position within it, is central to our understanding of modernity and modern life among new middle-class groups in Lahore.

PROGRESS, MODERNITY, AND THE NEW MIDDLE CLASS

In the new middle-class circles that I became familiar with, ideas on both modern life and *asl* Islam reflected the moral and class rhetoric described earlier, as well as the hierarchies and positions that are formed through them. Although almost all of them self-identified as simply "middle class," I have added the prefix of "new" here as a way to differentiate them from the established and old middle-class groups. Many of them were second-generation migrants. Bolstered by the benefits of Ayub's green revolution, they were from families that had migrated from smaller towns in Punjab in the late 1970s and 1980s, originally settling in areas on Ravi Road. Those who were richer had found homes in areas such as Samanabad, Muslim Town, Shah Jamal, and Saddar. Other families, however, had a much longer association with Lahore and belonged to groups that had been settled in the city for several generations. Such families had often originally lived in, or near, the walled city and, subsequently, following the general pattern of upward mobility described in Chapter 2, had moved to newer areas over successive generations. Some of them were first-generation migrants from small towns in Punjab, but had moved to Lahore after spending time abroad, either in the United States, United Kingdom, or the Persian Gulf states.

Most of them were of middling rank, employed as doctors in government hospitals, engineers, university lecturers, or owners of small businesses. In addition, a significant number held mid-level positions in the private sector, in national and multinational companies, and banks.

Although some of them had disposable incomes that were comparable to old middle-class groups, they did not possess the same kind of entrenched stability of established groups. Despite the significant generational progress that many of these families had made, they were vulnerable to setbacks caused by fluctuations in the economy and loss of jobs, or by the sudden death or illness of the main income provider. Moreover, as discussed earlier in this chapter, although wealth does matter, class positions need to be continually constructed and maintained through the social circles in which one moves, notably through the display of particular dispositions and tastes. This often involves suturing linkages with the past, notably the progressive history of the region, and exhibiting a deference to, and nostalgia for, old middle-class life. Associations of the past serve as bargaining chips in contestations for _khāndānī_ status, but their value depends on legitimacy and recognition from the outside world. As I explain below, although many contested the _khāndānī_ status of established groups, often by pointing out their lack of morality, most of them had neither the means nor the background to participate in such forms of self-display and representation. Moreover, not only did they predominantly move in different social circles from established groups, they often constructed their own identity in opposition to them.

A large number of families belonging to new middle-class circles live in residential areas and housing developments in the south of the city, such as Township and Allama Iqbal Town and other housing societies close to the Link and Canal Roads.[40] In particular, many of the families that I became familiar with lived in housing areas along or close to the canal. A number of these developments were cooperatives, made for the employees and families of particular government institutions and universities, such as WAPDA Town and Tech Society. Others, built more recently, have been constructed by private developers who were allowed to enter the housing market in the mid-1990s. Dotted along the Canal Road, many of them have foreign or Western names, such as Valencia Town, Lake City, and Orlando Town—reflective, perhaps, of the aspirations that they are trying to tap. For most of the families I interacted with, a move to these new housing developments came with a significant change in status. For some, after years of renting, it was a step up on the property ladder while, for others, it had meant a change from the joint to nuclear family system. Thus, most people were very proud of their houses, seeing them as both a symbol of success in their own lives and as a sign of broader generational progress and upward mobility.

While recounting their experiences, the progress they had made in their own lives and across generations, most drew upon the larger modernization narrative and emphasized the importance of education, hard work, and rational sensibilities.[41] Often, they would talk of the sacrifices that their parents or elders had made to ensure a good education for their children. For instance, a lecturer in engineering at the nearby university often mentioned that it was only through his parents' hard work and savings that he and his siblings had been able to reach the positions they currently enjoyed. His father had migrated to Lahore from a small town in northern Punjab in the early 1970s and worked as a low-level employee in a local government office. His income was modest but he invested it wisely, choosing to prioritize his children's education. "Both my father and mother, they wanted us to get ahead. . . . My father had only studied till matric, but he wanted us to go further," he explained.[42] Alongside his parents' sacrifices and planning for the future, my informant highlighted his own hard work. After getting a first division in his FSc. exams, he was able to get a place—"completely on merit" he emphasized—in the government-run engineering university where he stayed until his masters. After finishing his masters, he was able to get a lecturer position in the same university, a role he continues to occupy. When the university employees were offered land in a housing cooperative, he used all his savings and also borrowed money from his brother to buy two plots. He later sold one and used the money to build the house they now lived in. Just as his parents had worked hard to give their offspring a better life, the lecturer was proud that his own children had a better education than him. "I went to a small government school in Gulshan Ravi . . . no one even knows its name . . . but my children all went to good private schools like Beaconhouse."

Such life stories, with their reliance on a somewhat teleological narrative, were common in the groups that I frequented. They were told not just to me, an outsider who would ask specifically about the past, but often repeated to their children in order to remind them to work hard and to focus on academic studies. Paradoxically, however, these life stories coexisted with a wider sense of disillusionment and skepticism with the modernist promise of education. While reliving their own life progression through a modernization narrative and expressing pride in the ability to send their children to good schools, most of my informants also argued that education alone does not get you far in Pakistan. They maintained that the "system" around them was so corrupt that degrees and a culture of merit had no value. Rather, it was only money and connections that mattered. I heard numerous accounts and experiences of people applying for a deserved job or promotion, only to find that it was given to a less-qualified candidate who was related to or knew people "at the top." Parents would often complain that no matter how hard their children worked and the "number" they got in their exams, most of the seats in top universities and medical colleges went to the children and relatives of politicians and bureaucrats. These complaints conveyed the vulnerability and insecurity felt by many of my informants, and the difficulties they routinely faced in trying to progress in a "system" that was holding them back. Despite this skepticism, the emotional appeal of education was immense within these groups; the ability to send their children to good (increasingly, private schools) was seen as a symbol of personal success. Within such debates, concerns about admissions and performance in exams was a frequent topic.

While hard work and education were routinely evoked in personal trajectories of progress, equal emphasis was placed on fortune and luck—a sense that Allah had been kind to them. My informants would attribute whatever they had achieved to the grace of Allah. Without His blessing, nothing could be achieved no matter how much anyone tried. Their claims, here, are supported by the socioeconomic unevenness around them, a consequence of maldistributed economic growth and a lack of safety nets. In such a context, it is common to find that while some have been able to avail themselves of the limited opportunities for economic prosperity, others in the extended family and social networks have not been so lucky. Differences in economic and social standing between family members were rarely discussed explicitly, but were often present and visible in the background. There also existed a wider sense that there was no guarantee whether the prosperity achieved would last, and there were enough examples around of how a setback—such as death, illness, but also bad investments—could lead to a change in socioeconomic standing. Investment in property, for instance, was a common form of saving and supplementing existing income. In most cases, this did not mean the purchase of an existing plot or piece of land but reserving one in a housing society or commercial area, often referred to as "buying a file," with the intention of selling it for profit. There were considerable risks in this form of investment; there was the possibility not only that the file's value would not increase but also of fraud and embezzlement on the part of the developers. Several had lost significant savings in buying files for plots that they later found out never existed, or where the housing scheme was declared bankrupt before development work started.

Here, material and socioeconomic progress were closely associated with ideas on modernity and on becoming modern. In Urdu, the closest translation of "modern" is *jadīd*. Coming from the Arabic root word *jadd*, which literally means "to cut off," *jadīd* is usually understood as "fresh," "new," and "recent." In everyday speech, however, *jadīd* is predominantly used to signify contemporariness; for instance, *jadīd science* (modern science). Most Lahoris prefer to use the English word "modern," colloquially pronounced as *mādurn*. An Urdu word that is used interchangeably with "modern" is *taraqqī*, literally meaning "progress" or "advancement," and used to denote positive change over time. Modernity was lived and displayed through material progress, ranging from the larger life choices it offered, such as building a home and sending children to English-medium schools, to reoccurring desires of consuming items of technology, other luxury goods, and eating out in restaurants. The importance of consumption in experiencing "modernity" was often expressed in leisure activities. In evenings and at weekends and holidays in particular, many middle-class families frequented the growing number of Western-style shopping malls of Lahore which house international and local brands, as well as fast-food franchises, such as McDonalds and Kentucky Fried Chicken.

The consumption of this lifestyle was not only a way of experiencing modernity but also a marker of a distinct middle-class identity.[43] The leisure and shopping areas that my informants enjoyed distinguished them from those further down on the socioeconomic ladder. At the same time, however, the buying and spending choices in these spaces differentiated them from those higher above. Such negotiations would often play themselves out in particular conduct and spending behavior. In most cases, visits to these malls and environments were not for shopping per se but were treated as an outing, where the family would walk around and view the different shops. Such visits might include sitting in the food court area with perhaps an ice cream or a small snack. It was only in exceptional cases, for instance, for a specific occasion or for *iftār* in *Ramazān,* that a full meal was consumed in these restaurants. There was thus a voyeuristic element to these outings where it was the experience, familiarity, and knowledge of what was on offer, rather than its material consumption, that distinguished these middle-class families from those below. Many women often commented that they enjoyed the "modern atmosphere" of malls, and contrasted the space with less exclusive shopping areas where roaming around unaccompanied would be commonly viewed as suspect. For instance, a woman who managed a headscarves and 'abāyah shop in a mall, discussed further in Chapter 4, would often let her teenage daughters come with her in the evenings and stroll around unaccompanied. "In a *bazaar,* it would not be safe," she would say, "but here the atmosphere is not that bad."[44]

The same spaces, however, provoked a set of moral and financial anxieties. While many of my informants welcomed this experience of modernity, seeing it as indicative of personal success and socioeconomic mobility, they were equally concerned about not appearing "too modern." In this sense, being overly modern stood for a blind following of Western norms and values, which they associated with established and elite groups. This could be seen, for instance, in how most women were familiar with all the latest designer fashions but colored their judgment with a particular moral overtone, such as limiting the exposure of skin. Such moralizing often segued into a general sense of differentiation from the upper classes who they would imply were not only morally lax but frivolous with their money. My informants frequently commented on how the same products from shops in luxurious malls were available elsewhere in the city at a lower price. Most of them preferred to shop in bazaars and shops that offered these cheaper options. Their ability to find the "best" price for a product was seen as not only a sign of street smarts, but also of knowing the value of money more generally, qualities that differentiated them from groups below and above. A group of women that I became familiar with from *dars* gatherings would often go to an expensive department store in Lahore to view the crockery on display. Later they would visit the whole-sale goods market in Shahalmi, near the walled city, to look for iden-tical or similar pieces at a lower price. More recently, many of them had started to shop at the new hypermarts, such as Metro, that have opened up in Lahore.

Like socioeconomic success, individual morality was often positioned on an "axis of progress," with considerable emphasis on self-improvement and growth over time.[45] Moral refinement and growth, in this context, was often articulated through the idea of becoming a better Muslim. Similar to what Deeb and Harb have noted in Beirut, such a view was not limited to those who were actively engaged in religious pursuits.[46] Indeed, I often found that people who were not particularly observant expressed a desire to make more of an effort to learn and incorporate Islamic prac-tices in their lives. In this respect, many envisaged themselves as being more observant and knowledgeable in the future. Such ideas were some-times reflected in marriage choices, as I discovered in the case of Ahmed, a computer scientist in his early twenties. When his family was looking for a suitable match for him, Ahmed expressed a wish to marry someone who was "more Islamic than [him]."[47] He explained that although he was, at the moment, irregular in his prayers and did not make an effort to seek religious knowledge, he would like to in the future. Being with someone who was already engaged in similar pursuits would not only help him in becoming a better Muslim but it would also mean that that there would be less friction between them in the future. At a broader level, the overlap between moral growth and being a better Muslim was indicative of the openness in what constitutes as "Islamic," rather than a moral sphere dominated by Islam. For instance, any of the attributes that made a person morally refined—such as formal education, wisdom, a kind demeanor toward others, honesty—could also be explained as behavior that is sanc-tioned in Quran and Sunna.

The notion of the moral subject improving over time conveys not only a degree of linearity but also what Ewing has called an "illusion of whole-ness."[48] These aspects were often evoked by middle-class Lahoris them-selves, but were unreflective of the variety of, often opposing, sources that informed their ideas on Islamic practices and teachings. These included, for instance, compulsory Islamic studies in school and college, along with informal instructions from family and friends, newspapers, television, and, increasingly, social media. At the same time, many had been exposed to and, in varying degrees, were aware of the views of a range of piety-based movements and religio-political parties. In particular, during their college and university days, many young men and women had come in contact with the piety movement, the Tablighi Jamaat, and the political party, the Jamaat-e-Islami. Exposure to the latter had come largely from its student wing, the Islami Jamiat-e-Talaba (IJT). More recently, as discussed in the next chapter, many women from these neighborhoods had started attending *dars* (religious study circles) as well as taking more formal courses in Quran schools.

In this broader environment, ideas on Islam and Muslim life were often the subject of avid debate and discussion. It was frequently claimed that it was this reflection and discussion on the relevance of Islam in contemporary life that differentiated them from groups above and below them. Here, established groups of Lahore were depicted as having abandoned Islam, thinking it to be "backward" and "dated," while those lower down the socioeconomic hierarchy were viewed as blindly following rituals. Yet in differentiating themselves from others and in discussions of Islamic practices, most drew upon a variety of sources, often without lasting allegiance to any particular position. Contrary to the tendency in academic work of distinguishing between different kinds of religious movements and groups, classifying them, for instance, as pietest or Islamist, most drew on ideas and discourses from both kinds of movements. Even when a particular religious group was supported, it did not signify an easy overlap between individual opinions and official stances and agendas. Rather, I found that support for a particular group was often issue-based, and open to shifts with changing circumstances over time.

This is visible in the example of Taimur, who had been intermittently involved with the Jamiat-e-Talaba when he was in his early twenties. At the time, Taimur had been in a government college, studying for his FA and BA. He had lost his father some years earlier from a sudden heart attack, an event that not only had been emotionally difficult but had also put the family under considerable financial strain. His education since then had been supported by extended family members, and he had obtained a partial scholarship for his FA. His association with the Jamiat began at the end of his first year in college, when he and his friends had a fight with another group of boys in college. It had started over something small but had quickly escalated; one of the boys in the opposing group was the son of a politician, a member of the provincial assembly, and had threatened to use his connections to get Taimur and his friends expelled. Activists from Jamiat-e-Talaba came to their rescue, and negotiated on their behalf with the other group to let the matter drop. Recounting the incident, Taimur mentioned that although he had always known that the Jamiat built their reputation through this kind of work, this was the first time that he fully realized its value and importance. "Middle-class boys like us ... with no connections, no father with clout ... nobody else would have come to our rescue but them."[49] After this incident, he became familiar with some IJT activists, and started to attend the organized events, both at his campus and other colleges in Lahore. Although he never formally joined either the student organization or the main party, he regularly attended their rallies and was, in particular, sympathetic to their agenda of social justice and equality. "This is essentially what Islam is about, justice and equality; all these _khāndānī_ people can talk all they want about being progressive and modern, but it's Islam that sets the foundation for a modern life where everyone is equal."[50]

However, while Taimur remained sympathetic to Jamiat on issues of justice and equality, he was ambivalent about their larger agenda of gaining political power to reform society. Recalling his experience with Jamiat activists, he said that the problem with trying to gain political power was that it was difficult not to get affected by it. In the Jamiat, he found, that some of the activists were always concerned with building a reputation.

> There is a stereotype of Jamiat being filled with gangsters ... people who are not interested in Islam, just like having power and throwing their weight around. That is not a true picture ... most of the activists are very committed. But this kind of political work, it has all kinds of negative effects on people. At first, someone joins the Jamiat because they believe in its vision ... so they get involved in its mission, helping others,

rallies ... all of these things are means to an end, to ultimately establish an Islamic system. But it is not always easy to remember that and sometimes people just become concerned with getting power.

For Taimur, this was not a problem with Jamiat activists alone but with most people in this world. He believed that it was part of human nature to be tempted by popularity and power. "The people in the Jamiat want to change society, but when they try to get into power ... in the process they change themselves." Here, he drew upon the notion of *nafs*, the Quranic concept of ego or soul, and talked about the need to control one's impulses and desires.[51] "This is the only way for a person and society to change ... to move forward," he said, "by controlling our instincts and encouraging others to do the same." Continuing, he said, "In politics, it is hard to do this—how can you tell others to be good Muslims when you are failing to control your own weaknesses." In his critique here, Taimur explained his position through his own observations and perspectives. The concept of *nafs* that he evoked is an important component of personhood in Muslim South Asia, and is drawn upon in a range of traditional piety-based movements, such as the Tablighi Jamaat, as well as by new Quran schools, discussed in the next chapter. However his use of these discourses did not mean complete support of any of these movements. Rather, it was a way for him to explain his own position vis-à-vis different religious groups, but also within the larger social and moral world.

Taimur's reflections and, in particular, his use of discourses from differing sources echo some of Humeira Iqtidar's work on the consequences of competition between religious groups. Focusing on Islamist organizations in Lahore, she argues that competition among these groups have engendered a "certain consciousness about the different paths towards a pious life."[52] Related to this, she found that, following in line with the larger objectification of Muslim practice, this kind of competition had initiated a process of rationalization, encouraging individuals to "define the 'right' religious package for themselves."[53] Some of the trends that she describes are visible in Taimur's perspectives and in discussions on Islam in new middle-class circles more generally. The exposure to different kinds of religious groups and their ideologies, along with easier access to Islamic texts and information, has led to increased discussion and debate on matters of practice and belief. This was certainly noticeable in the conversation described above, where Taimur drew upon his experience of different groups and the discourses that he had encountered to give an opinion on pious life. Iqtidar found that the debate fostered by competition encouraged a degree of doctrinal promiscuity, in that there was noticeable switching between groups. The interactions in my setting revealed that discourses and arguments from different sources were used simultaneously, often with sympathy toward multiple positions and without lasting affiliation to any. Here, the focus was often on debate and deliberation in itself, and on using these differing discourses to draw out the continuing relevance of Islam not only in an individual's life but also in the contemporary world more broadly.

I discuss in the next chapter whether these trends can be seen, as Iqtidar does, as part of a broader process of rationalization. For now, however, the point that I want to focus on is that these discussions of Islam were situated within the broader moral world of new middle-class groups. In other words, ideas on Islam were not only reflective of their position within larger moral and social hierarchies, but also understood in relation to wider class relations. This was visible, for instance, in the way Taimur's views were contextualized in relation to those considered above him and those below in the class hierarchy. Moreover, his discussion allowed him to question the moral position of those above him. As described in this chapter, moral and social hierarchies are maintained and navigated through discourses of modernization and progress, and through an appeal to the notion of *asl* Islam. In this context, discussions of Islam—what it means to be a good Muslim and to lead a pious life—are part of larger aspirations for moving forward, both in terms of personal trajectories of upward mobility and in relation to wider class and moral hierarchies. It is in this context that the next chapter explores the growing trends toward piety in these new middle-class and upwardly mobile groups.

THREE

Piety and New Middle-Class Life

IT WAS FRIDAY AFTERNOON in Lahore and Amina *bājī* and I had collected her children from school and were rushing home. The afternoon *Jum'a* prayer was ending soon and we wanted to avoid the traffic produced by worshippers leaving their mosques. As we waited at a traffic light near the school, with the car windows rolled down, we could hear parts of the sermon from a nearby mosque. Upon hearing the *khaṭīb* (preacher) direct the men not to allow their women out of the house, Amina *bājī* exclaimed angrily, "Just look at him, he has probably never opened the Book to see what's written, just repeating what another *jāhil* said."[1] It is common in Pakistan, and in the Muslim world more broadly, to find people casting doubt on the ability and intentions of established religious authorities—the figure of the *maulā'ī*, in particular, has long been a subject of jokes and derision.[2] Amina *bājī's* criticism, however, came from a particular perspective. The *khaṭīb's* misogynistic remarks had made her angry, but she placed the blame on his supposed inability (or lack of desire) to independently read and understand the Quran. Like a growing number of urban men and women in Pakistan, Amina *bājī* placed great importance on reading and understanding the Quran for oneself. After finishing her medical degree,

she had enrolled in a local Quran school to read the Quran with translation and commentary. Amina *bājī* had a demanding routine: in the
morning, she served as the resident doctor at a local boarding school, and
the rest of her day was preoccupied with looking after the house and her
three school-age children. Despite this busy schedule, she managed to host
a weekly religious study circle *(dars)*, where she would read different verses
of the Quran and their commentary with her companions.

This chapter examines the religious sensibility, noticeable in new
middle-class groups, that privileges the personal study of Quran, the
points of reference and authority that it appeals to, and its engagement
with discourses of science and rationality. My focus, here, is not on the
intended outcome of such a form of ethical self-cultivation in the construction of an ideal virtuous self. Rather, the discussion pivots around the
ways in which pious women talk about this pursuit, the wider discourses
that they evoke when explaining their comments and the dilemmas and
pressures that they face. Carrying forward a theme from the previous
chapter, I draw attention to the instances in which this pursuit overlaps
with, and when it causes tensions with aspirations for, upward mobility
and social recognition. My focus here is on new middle-class groups—
not least because this is the demographic where this kind of religious
sensibility is most evident, but also because it allows us to understand
how new forms of piety bring together a variety of aspirations relating to
desires for progress and modernity. The first section of the chapter illustrates the broader environment in which these women turned toward a
personal study of the Quran and the reasons that they give for their commitment. Following from this discussion, the second section explores the
popularity of neighborhood *dars* gatherings, and their connections with
Islamic practices in the West. The third section turns to a deeper understanding of how new middle-class groups have a broader engagement
with discourses of "global" Islam. The final section considers the role of
choice, authority, and rationalization in this form of personalized piety.

A TURN TO ISLAM

One afternoon, as we were having tea in her living room, Amina *bājī*
reflected on how she had decided to join a Quran school. Ever since she

was a teenager, she had a desire to read the Quran with commentary. "In my family, all around me, I always heard people talking about Islam and what the Quran says, so it was only natural that I was curious to know what it actually says," she explained.[3] At that time, however, she had neither the time nor sufficient motivation. "Life is very simple when you are that age," she mused, "for me, everything revolved around getting the numbers [marks] to get into medical college. Then when I got in, it was about passing those exams. That was my goal." After she married and became busy with raising her children, she realized that, outside of looking after her family, she did not have any goals that were for herself alone.

> Looking after your family is so important and it takes away so much of your time—when my children were little, there were days when I felt like I did not get time to go the washroom [bathroom]. Then as they started going to school, it was about dropping and picking them up from school, making them study and get good *marks*. You worry whether you are doing enough or they need tuition. But in all of this, you sometimes feel empty, not like yourself. That is when I started thinking of how do I make my life have a goal, make it meaningful. When I joined [the Quran school] and focused on the Quran, I knew in my heart that I had found my goal.

The residential colony that Amina *bājī* lived in was relatively new. Located along the canal, it is one of several private and public residential developments in the area that cater to the expanding middle-class population of Lahore. As explained in Chapter 2, most of the families who live in these developments are of middling rank. As schoolteachers, traders, businessmen, doctors, and middle-ranking employees of national and multinational companies, many of them are part of the new middle class of Lahore. This was certainly the case with the families settled in Amina *bājī's* neighborhood, where most of the men were often employed in mid-level positions, predominantly in the private sector, particularly banks as well as small businesses. Some of them were doctors, employed in government hospitals. The majority of women did not work, although most had at least a bachelors degree and several had finished postgraduate education. Those who did work were employed as teachers in primary and secondary-level schools or in corporate offices in the private sector. In most cases, the move to these housing developments was seen as a culmination of years of hard work and sacrifice—a significant move forward in terms of personal trajectories of upward mobility. For instance, before moving to this house, Amina bājī had lived in Shah Jamal with a joint family, including her parents-in-law and her husband's elder brother and his family. They had been able to acquire a house in this development by selling a plot that her husband had inherited from his parents and by taking out a housing loan, given to mid-level employees, at the private bank where he worked.

Most people were proud of their house, seeing it as a symbol of how far they had come from their origins. Women, in particular, would make significant effort to decorate and maintain their homes. Similarly, many also considered it a sign of personal success that, while they had predominantly attended local government schools, they could now afford to send their offspring to better—often private—institutions. At the same time, both these symbols of personal progress were also sources of considerable anxiety and concern. Complaints about ever-increasing prices and inflation were common, including worries about paying bills and school fees, whilst maintaining their desired standard of living. The quality of education that their children were receiving was an enduring concern. Young mothers, in particular, were always anxious about the performance of their children in school and, subsequently, would worry about their future prospects. Many of these women often spent at least a couple of hours on the road every day, dropping off and collecting children at school and, sometimes, tuition centers.

Like Amina *bājī*, most women—even those who did not work—had considerable demands on their time. Alongside the school runs and child-caring duties, they were also responsible for managing the house, cooking and buying daily groceries. Despite this routine, many echoed the lack of purpose and emptiness that Amina *bājī* described, and explained that it was this feeling that had led them to the path of Allah and Islam. For instance, Nina, a young mother who lived in the same neighborhood, told me,

I suppose there was nothing to my life. On the surface I was busy all the time, but inside I felt very purposeless. I woke up in the morning, made breakfast, dropped the children to school, picked them up and helped with homework. One day while driving home, I just thought, is that all there is to my life? What is the meaning of this? It was then that I turned to Allah.[4]

It was this feeling of purposelessness that motivated Nina to start regularly attending the *dars* gathering that Amina *bājī* organized. When I met Nina, it had been almost two years since she had started going for *dars.* "I feel that my life has more value now, that I put my mind and efforts towards something higher," she said, "otherwise, it was always the same worries, about money and expenses, children's school." Referring to the *dars,* she continued "now we can come together to make ourselves grow on the inside."

Alongside a sense of purposeless, many spoke of a feeling of isolation in their daily lives. Both men and women often lamented that although their family members lived in the same city, sometimes less than half an hour away, they did not meet them as much as they would like. They frequently mentioned how, when they were young, they had been surrounded by family, but this was not the case for their children. Such comments reflected the changes that had come, at least for some of them, with the move from joint to nuclear family living. Moreover, it spoke of the responsibilities that came with their aspired lifestyle, the worries and anxieties that they now wrestled with, and the demands on their time. Women, in particular, would often complain that after they were done with the housework and school-related duties, they had little time to socialize. And, even when they did have time to meet their family and friends, it felt rushed and not as relaxing as it used to be. For comparison, they would narrate idyllic stories of their younger days. For instance, Fareeha often mentioned that she and her sister were exceptionally close when growing up but now, even though they lived only a few miles away from each other, they never had the time to meet. "When we were younger, we were always together. . . . We shared a room and the whole night we would be whispering to each other. Now we talk on the phone, but sometimes weeks go by and we don't meet."[5]

Comparisons with the past were made not only to emphasize the change in the pace of life, but also to highlight differences in priorities and values. While my informants were proud of the progress that they had made in recent decades, they would, at the same time, often present the past as "a better time" *(běhtar waqt)*. Relying on a somewhat idealized narration of the past, they claimed that, when they were younger, they were surrounded by the right values and principles. Reminiscing about such days, they contended that people cared about their families and friends, and derived happiness and value from such relationships. In contrast, in contemporary society, life tended to privilege money and material gains. It was on this basis that people lived their lives—compassion, honor, and integrity were all things of the past. My informants lamented that, inevitably, they too were becoming the embodiment of such material values. As Nina's earlier comments indicate, many people felt that their anxieties and worries were imbued with material concerns and that they did little else in their lives.

In this context, my informants often saw their commitment to Islamic learning as a way of moving beyond their material concerns and finding deeper meaning in their lives. With much of their time and effort spent on maintaining their standard of living and investing in the future, many felt a need to concentrate on, as Nina described it, "growing from the inside." As I just explained, much of the focus on this form of religiosity is on making an active and conscious commitment to leading a pious life. Yet descriptions of how people had come to realize this often evoked the sense that they had been led to this point through their life experiences and the unforeseen will of Allah. Similarly, while much of this discourse of piety centers around knowing the significance behind Islamic practices—of employing one's critical faculties—it was common to find people mentioning that they had been led by their heart and emotions. For instance, in her narration of how her sense of purposelessness had led her to Islam, Amina *bājī* had known "in her heart" that this was the right path. Before it, her heart had been restless and unsatisfied *(dil nahīṅ lagtā)*. Another woman, who had just started attending a Quran school, said that she had never thought that she would be interested in seeking religious knowledge. "Then," she explained, "one day, on a friend's insistence, I went with her to a *dars* gathering. . . . The woman giving it was

from Karachi, and was famous for her *dars*. Her voice, her message, everything was so beautiful, I had never felt this kind of *sukūn* (peace) in my
heart before."[6] After this episode, she knew that she had to seek Islamic
knowledge.

For others, the decision to embark on this path was linked to personal
experiences, particularly related to loss and bereavement. In moments of
emotional stress and grief, many felt the need to find deeper meaning in
their lives and discovered themselves drawn to Allah. As Sajida, an inter-
locutor who started attending *dars* after her mother died of cancer,
explained,

> When *Ammi* died, I needed solace and I found it in Allah. But even
> before that, I always had this curiosity about [the] Quran. At home, we
> just venerate this book, put it in a high place out of respect but we don't
> bother to really open it. . . . I kept thinking I will read it with meaning
> one day, but never found time for it. But then, with *Ammi's* illness, I could
> not find peace anywhere until I opened the Quran, and really started
> understanding it.[7]

Similarly, many had turned to the Quran after the untimely death of a
sibling or, in particular, a child. One of the dars gatherings that I attended
in the residential area of Garden Town was hosted by Nuzhat, a woman
who had lost her five-year-old daughter in a car accident. She told me
that, following their daughter's death, her husband had become removed
and distant from everyone and took no interest in anything. On the advice
of a friend, he started praying regularly and asked his wife to do the same.
"*Nāmāz* changed us both, it taught us *sabr* (patience)," she said.[8] Some
months later she started attending *dars* and, over the years, began hosting
her own sessions. In such instances, although the decision had been personal, it was accompanied with a sense that they had been led there by the
circumstances they had faced and through some inexplicable feeling that
this was the right path. Often, people would mention that in moments of
doubt and uncertainty, their commitment was renewed by a sign or an
incident. For instance, when she had first started praying regularly, Nuzhat
sometimes had moments when she wondered why she was doing this,
and if it could help her deal with her loss. She only became convinced

after she had dreams in which she saw her daughter happy and smiling. Before this, she regularly dreamed of her daughter, but would always see images of her in distress or injured. Nuzhat interpreted the new dreams as a sign that she was finally doing something right. "Now," she once told me, "I feel that I had to, through this tragedy, realize what is [the] real and right path."[9] Others, who had turned to Islam after a loss or tragedy argued that such experiences brought out the meaninglessness of the material world and opened a door for them to recognize a deeper truth.

On the one hand, a commitment to cultivating Islamic values was viewed as transcending material concerns and anxieties associated with middle-class lifestyles, while also providing the means for reflecting and moving beyond personal hardships and tragedies. On the other hand, it was simultaneously connected to ideas on worldly progress. In this context, acquiring religious knowledge and cultivating the right ethics were considered keys for moving forward, both in terms of moral growth and for attaining material success. Moreover, it was believed that Islamic values held the answer to problems holding Pakistan back from "moving forward" to become a "modern" nation. Such ideas are, of course, reminiscent of the broader discourse surrounding *asl* Islam discussed in Chapter 2. For Amina *bājī* and a growing number of people in the expanded middle class of Lahore, the way to *asl* Islam was through a personal engagement with the Quran and other Islamic texts. By attending *dars* gatherings or Quran schools, their aim was to understand the meaning of Allah's message in its purest form, without relying on intermediaries, and to use that knowledge to cultivate Islamic ethics in their daily lives. Here, significant importance was placed both on following Islamic tenants and on using one's critical faculties—developed through education—in understanding the reason for, and relevance of such practices.

For many people, this kind of engagement with the Quran was not only viewed as the path to *asl* Islam, but was often considered as a sign of being middle-class in itself. They claimed that it was this commitment, to use available resources and skills developed through education, to understand the Quran that distinguished them from groups above and below. Such ideas drew upon local class distinctions, while also referencing the larger position of Muslims in the contemporary world and, in particular, in relation to the West. As I describe in the following section, references

to an abstract West were a way of both reflecting upon local class positions and demonstrating connections and knowledge with the outside
world. The local, in this context, often played out on a global stage.

LOCAL ANXIETIES AND THE WEST

Often, ideas on "moving forward"—and connections between cultivating
ethics through the personal study of the Quran —surfaced in conversations
about what it means to live a modern life and, in particular, to be a modern
Muslim. In turn, such discussions relied upon an opposition; that is, being
modern was explained through what it was not. Equally, it usually involved
a subversion of conventionally held hierarchies, where established groups
are deemed more "modern" than groups lower down the socioeconomic
ladder. One evening, as I was sitting with a group of women after a *dars*,
our discussion turned to the topic of modernity. Leena, a schoolteacher in
her late thirties mentioned that she was often worried for her daughter,
who had recently got a scholarship to do her A Levels at a prestigious
private school. "*Studies-wise*, it is the best but I worry about the environment," she said.[10] Referring to the other students, many of whom came
from well-known backgrounds, she continued, "you know what children
from *baṛe gharāne* (lit. "big households") are like, what their ways are . . . no
moral guidance in their lives. I do not want Mahnoor [her daughter] to
come *under pressure* and become like that." Seema, another regular attendee
at these *dars* sessions, added in agreement. "Yes, these worries are always
there, especially when they [children] are at an impressionable age." She
then reflected, "The real problem with these *liberals* is that they think that
being modern is about wealth, wearing fashionable clothes—that you do
whatever they are doing in the West."[11] Annie, who had been listening to
the conversation, added, "Yes, they are just interested in *show*, they don't
realize that all these degrees and education [are] worth nothing if we do
not put them to the right use. . . . You develop your mind to guide you
towards Allah."[12] Leena nodded in agreement,

> They always think we are *backward*, but it is because they have no idea
> what the Quran really says. They think it oppresses us women because
> they cannot tell religion apart from culture. It gives more allowances than

even liberalism.... Islam is so modern and relevant but they look at someone with a covered head and think she is *backward*.

There are several themes running through this discussion that eluci-date the ways in which the women at this gathering located their pious commitments within wider concerns about class positions and ideas on modernity. First, for the women participating in this conversation, being modern was equated with "developing the mind." Here, their views echoed the class rhetoric inflected with modernism, discussed in Chapter 2, where rationality and education—evidence of being modern—were a gauge for social hierarchies. Their opinions here were reflective not only of the immense appeal of education in Pakistan but also of the disap-pointment in its promise not being fully realized. A parallel example can be found across the border in India, where educational qualifications are often a way for marginalized groups to assert themselves as "developed people" or "civilized." [13] Yet despite gaining the requisite degrees, many college graduates are unable to find appropriate jobs and to achieve the socioeconomic mobility to which they aspire. Such frustrations resonate with the experiences of many new middle-class families who, despite the progress they have made, felt vulnerable and held back by a corrupt, nep-otistic system. Moreover, as Leena's remarks suggested, many of them felt that, even though they were educated and had made significant economic progress, they were perceived as "backward" and uncultured by estab-lished groups. In turn, they too argued that educational qualifications or family background—qualities that established families associated with themselves—were not enough to be considered modern. Rather, taking it a step further, they argued it required employing the faculties developed through education to study the Quran. This way of thinking challenged the modernism-inflected class rhetoric deployed by established groups. At the same time, however, it revealed a sensibility shaped by the mod-ernism of mass education, in that Islam (and religion more broadly) was treated as a distinct sphere of study that could be understood through utilizing the right methods. I return to this theme in the next section.[14]

Equally, it is noticeable how, in this discussion, they pitted their views against an idea of a modernism to which they did not ascribe. Similar to the case of most conversations on modernity in Lahore, it was directed toward an audience that perceived Lahoris, and Pakistan more broadly, as "backward." In this particular context, we started with an (imagined) audience which featured the more privileged families associated with a private school. The differences between these two groups were of class and socioeconomic security but, much like the upper-class critique of emerging groups, they were articulated through a discourse of rationality and morality. However, as this conversation progressed, the audience lost its specificity and any distinct markers were flattened out by the use of the generic category of "liberals." This term was used derogatorily to refer to the established circles in Lahore, but it encompassed a broader stance and attitude toward Islam and Muslims that my informants associated with an abstract West. A shift from localized tensions to general anxieties about global self-representation was a common move in most discussions about modernity at *dars* gatherings and, more broadly, in pious middle-class circles. Reflections on what it means to be a modern Muslim requires the presence of an imagined audience, but one that seamlessly transitions from the local setting to a global stage.

This audience is, of course, constructed in the sense that it is neither fully representative of established *khāndānī* families, nor does it capture the range of sociopolitical values and attitudes prevalent in the West. As discussed in Chapter 2, there is considerable debate and contestation over what it means to be *khāndānī*, and while some appeal to family background and education, others, much like the women at this gathering, construct it in relation to values and style of comportment. Similarly, while the discussants at this gathering critiqued privileged families for not using their *'aql* (critical faculties) to understand Islam, many established families level the same accusations against pious middle-class groups, and complain that they are blindly following Saudi Arabia's Wahhabism. And, although the mainstream press and media outlets are often critical of Muslim attitudes and norms, there is no singular liberal position on the place of Muslims, and religious groups more broadly, in Western countries.

Rather than revealing something about the audience, its presence in conversations on modernity, reveals more about the general anxieties about self-representation on the part of my informants. More importantly, it offers a window on the scales of references through which they viewed themselves. Although the feeling of marginality that was visible in their discussions stemmed from more immediate everyday class tensions, it was subsumed within a larger sense of Muslims being peripheral on the "global" stage. Like the established groups that derive their status from connections with, and knowledge of the outside world, most people in new middle-class circles showed an avid interest in global affairs and politics—a trend that has only increased with the exponential growth of private news channels in Pakistan. They were particularly interested in news about the fate of Muslims elsewhere in the world. The position of Palestinians in Israel, and the tacit acceptance of such conditions by the United States and European countries, was often a point of discussion. Equally, my informants would bring up the brutal treatment of prisoners in U.S. detention camps. They would argue that the reason why other countries and international organizations, such as the United Nations, allowed such activity to continue was because all the prisoners were Muslims—and often from poor countries—and nobody seriously cared about how they were treated or even if they received due process.

As much as they blamed non-Muslim countries for discriminatory policies, most were also critical of Muslims for allowing themselves to be in these conditions. They blamed leaders and the elite of Muslim states for making alliances with Western countries for their own narrow interests, with little regard for how such alliances affected common people. Equally, they felt that ordinary Muslims were at fault for not standing up for what was right, and for not stepping out of their own problems to see what was going on around them. Throughout the world, they argued, Muslims were seen as "backward" people and Islam as a religion of fanaticism and violence. Wherever they looked, they found that Muslims were stigmatized for their presumed irrationality and lack of desire to progress and "move forward." My informants would mourn that Islam had this "global" image because Muslims did not make an effort to understand what their religion actually preached and to show it to the world through their conduct. By understanding the guidance offered in the Quran, and employing it in their daily lives, my informants wanted the larger world to see the rationality inherent in Allah's message. It was this global perspective, and the embarrassment which accompanied it, that gave my informants a sense of cultural intimacy, as well as a lens for reflecting upon their own

social position locally and the tensions and problems that came with
such visions.

At the same time, the seamless transition to a global stage and knowledge about the Muslim world beyond Pakistan offered a way of rising above
their local context and positioning. The interest in the situation of Muslims
worldwide was paralleled with a curiosity about Islamic practices beyond
Pakistan. In particular, discussions on Muslim life and the difficulties faced
in practicing Islam in the West were a common point of conversation.
Aware of the growing levels of Islamophobia and incidences of racial discrimination, most were admired the effort that the Muslims in the West
made to lead pious lives. Many of my interlocutors felt that in a Muslim
country like Pakistan, people did not have to make an effort to follow
Islamic guidelines; for instance, they were served halal food wherever they
went, the sound of the *azān* told them when to pray, and state holidays
marked auspicious days and events. As a result, they held the view that most
people did not even have to think about being Muslim. In contrast, those in
the West had to make a conscious decision to lead a Muslim life, and that
it required constant dedication. In this regard, what impressed them the
most was how this commitment led them to acquire knowledge about
Islam through personal inquiry and learning.

As mentioned earlier, in Pakistan, like in other non-Arabic Muslim
countries, reading the Quran in Arabic takes precedence over reading it
in the local language. Most people thus read the Quran in Arabic and,
until recently, few have proceeded to read a translation or a commentary.
Among my informants who attended *dars,* this was often cited as an
example of the lack of interest of most Pakistanis in understanding what
Islam was about. Comparing them with Muslims who lived abroad, they
would mention that children there were taught the "Quran with meaning"
in Islamic centers and how, during *Ramazān,* they would attend special
classes to learn more about why Allah commands his people to fast and
its relevance in contemporary life. My informants were of the belief that
this emphasis on learning meant that Muslims abroad took the trouble to
understand the meaning behind Islamic prescriptions and, thus, followed
such prescriptions in their "true" form. In Pakistan, they lamented that
people just practice what they see others do, with no reflection or learning,
and have no idea what is Islam and what is culture.

These opinions have been shaped not only through consumption of media and stories on Muslim life in the West, but also through the exchange of information with family relations and friends living abroad. As discussed in Chapter 2, there has been substantial migration to the West—mainly Britain and United States—as well as the Gulf among both established and emerging urban groups in Lahore. The latter did not come from well-established families, but were able to study in state-subsidized medical colleges and engineering universities, and use their education to emigrate to the United States. Although, in some cases, the employment they found did not match their skill level, it allowed them a somewhat comfortable standard of living. Many of the families that I knew through *dars* gatherings, and in new middle-class circles more broadly, had friends and relatives abroad who fell in this category. In addition, in some cases, their relatives had traveled to the United States as semi-skilled laborers—in particular, working as taxi drivers and in restaurants—and later progressed enough to own small businesses or shops. Communication and interaction with them, through phone calls, social media, and occasional visits, was a source of information about Muslim life in the West. Moreover, in a number of cases, many of these friends and family members abroad had started attending Islamic centers. They often shared these experiences of "global" Islam with their family and friends at home. Such connections and exchange of information were further augmented through return-migration in this group. Although this was not as substantial as migration from Pakistan, there was considerable movement back, in particular, due to a need to care for elderly parents or a desire to familiarize children with life in Pakistan and to find suitable matches for them.

Drawing upon such connections abroad allowed my informants to construct themselves as part of a "global" Muslim community, an identity that is often as abstracted as the "West," and one which they frequently pit themselves against. Such an abstraction, however, allows new middle-class groups to bypass the old elite and the middle class—groups that typically control access to a world outside Pakistan—and assert themselves on a global stage. Text is paramount to this form of representation; to read, analyze, and understand the Quran is fundamental in claiming a modern Muslim identity. In the following section, I focus on *dars* gatherings to highlight the centrality of text in cultivating ethics, and in making an active commitment to lead a pious life. Such a form of piety draws upon and engages with "global" Islam but, at the same time, often generates debate and discussion that challenges its predominance.

DARS, KNOWLEDGE, AND "GLOBAL" ISLAM

Dars sessions are usually held once a week in the home one of the participants and are led by a woman skilled in Quranic exegesis. There are, however, some Quran schools that also host *dars* gatherings, particularly in *Ramaẓān*, to cater to women who are not enrolled in any of their regular courses but, nevertheless, have an interest in learning. In each session, some verses of the Quran, and the context in which they were revealed, are translated and explained, often using everyday examples. This is followed by a more general discussion, focused on the relevance of these verses in daily lives as well as the broader sociopolitical context. In *Ramaẓān*, it is common for the sessions to become more frequent and intense, with the aim of finishing the entire Quran within the month. Most *dars* sessions are informal and relaxed. At Amina *bājī's* house, for instance, other women often brought their children, who would play together in a separate room, but frequently came inside to talk to their mothers. The women who attended this *dars* all knew each other and felt comfortable interrupting Amina *bājī* to ask questions and often laughed at the jokes that she sometimes cracked. Other arrangements are more formal and require the audience to adopt a more serious tone for the duration. In a *dars* that I once attended in a neighboring residential area, I was told beforehand that the *dars*-giver expected simplicity in attire and did not permit children to allow for participants to concentrate. In this particular case, the *dars*-giver was a teacher in a local Quran school who had been asked by the hostess to hold a weekly session at her house for the women in her close family and the neighborhood.

Today, *dars* is predominantly associated with individualized piety and a desire to cultivate personal ethics, but this was not always the case. In the late 1960s and early 1970s, the Jamaat-e-Islami, the country's largest religious and political party, organized *dars* sessions, but attendance was confined to party members and sympathizers. In the 1980s, during General

Zia-ul-Haq's rule by martial law, college and university campuses were dominated by the student wing of the Jamaat-e-Islami, the Jamiat, which organized *dars* in male and female student hostels.[15] As a result, *dars* became more frequent and included young people but, at the same time, remained connected with a particular political position and were not part of mainstream society. *Dars* became more popular in the early 1990s through the efforts of Dr. Farhat Hashmi, who, at the time, was a lecturer at the International Islamic University in Islamabad. Born in Sargodha, a district in Punjab, Hashmi was the daughter of an Islamic scholar closely associated with the Jamaat-e-Islami and, as a young girl, she had accompanied her parents to many *dars* lessons organized by the party.[16] Her skills at giving *dars* can be attributed to this history, but her success and popularity is linked more to her doctorate in Hadith Sciences from the University of Glasgow in Britain, and her experience of lecturing and preaching Islam in the West, a point that I will return to below.[17] As she gained popularity at *dars* gatherings, she opened Al-Huda, an Islamic school for women offering diploma courses in Quran and Islamic studies. The school has subsequently expanded and now has branches in different cities. Offering diploma courses in Quranic exegesis and Islam, the school has acquired a degree of popularity in Pakistan and, moreover, has opened branches in other countries.

In the English-language press, whose circulation is largely confined to the upper and established urban classes, Al-Huda has often been labeled an "elite school."[18] Such a description is only partially, if at all, accurate. Many of these news stories report that the *dars* gatherings led by Farhat Hashmi attract women from affluent backgrounds, yet they tell us little about their social positioning in relation to other urban groups. From my own experience at Al-Huda in Lahore, I found that, with few exceptions, none of the students came from the established or well-known Lahori families. The institutions largely attracted teachers and students from new middle-class families. Some of them were, in relative terms, financially comfortable, while others relied on the generous and wide-reaching fee waivers offered by Al-Huda. Moreover, the school has popularized the idea of a Quran school in new middle-class circles and many similar schools have opened up in different neighborhoods in Lahore. Al-Huda also encourages its scholars to spread the message of Islam after they have finished the diploma. Many graduates become teachers at the school or give *dars* lessons in their family circles and among friends. Thus, while Al-Huda and *dars* gatherings have become a general feature of urban life in Lahore, they have made deeper inroads in new middle-class families than in established and *khāndānī* circles.

At a broader level, the coverage of Al-Huda and *dars* gatherings in the English-language press reflects the general disdain among liberal groups of Islam in the urban public sphere. As discussed in Chapter 1, there is a tendency within these circles to derogatorily label all kinds of Islamic parties and groups—ranging from the Jamaat-e-Islami and the Deobandi Jamiat Ulema-e-Islam to the Tablighi Jamaat and Dawat-e-Islami—as Wahhabi. As a result, the new religious trends of building a textual and personal understanding of Islam are predictably perceived as a sign of the growing influence of Saudi Arabia and the Gulf states. Within such a portrayal, Al-Huda and Quran schools are lumped together with all other parties and groups that are commonly labeled "Wahhabi," and blamed for the loss of Sufi-inspired pluralism in Pakistani society. Along with supporters of other religious groups who veil or wear their beards long, women who attend Quran schools are often negatively labeled by liberal circles as *fundō* (short for "fundamentalist") or as *ninja* (in reference to their covered faces). Moreover, in both the English-language press and among liberal groups, supporters of these different religious organizations are often portrayed as idealizing Saudi Arabia, and Arabic language and culture more broadly.

However, while its critics tend to view Al-Huda as indistinguishable from other Wahhabi groups, its appeal for its followers lies precisely in the sense that it is unlike other local religious movements and parties. When discussing the merits of attending a Quran school or *dars* gathering, many of my informants explained their commitment as a desire to seek knowledge that was devoid of any political associations or sectarian leanings. They claimed that this was what made their Quran school or *dars* different from other religious organizations and groups which they, in turn, believed either propagated their own political interests or promoted the views of a particular sect. For instance, my informants emphasized that the translation and exegesis at Al-Huda explained "word for word" what the Quran says and never extended beyond such a conclusion. As one informant put

it, "What you get at Al-Huda is *pure knowledge* about what Allah's message is."[19] Similarly, others argued that the teachers at Al-Huda explained
what the Quran said "nothing less and nothing more" and then left it to
the person how to interpret and apply such ideas. My informants from
Al-Huda rarely talked about Dr. Farhat Hashmi's association with the
Jamaat-e-Islami. On the exceptional occasions when the connection arose,
they differentiated between Maulana Mawdudi's scholarly work—his
Quranic exegesis in Urdu, they would argue, is one of the best—and his
political legacy as founder of Jamaat-e-Islami. In contrast to the silence on
the Jamaat-e-Islami, they would frequently mention her doctorate in
Hadith Sciences from a foreign university, which they saw not only as
proof of her extensive knowledge but also as evidence of sectarian neu-
trality. It was important to build a direct relationship with the text, one
that was not contaminated by the politics and the sectarian affiliations
they associated with other local religious organizations.

Similarly, at *dars* gatherings, most participants emphasized the neu-
trality of their commitment, arguing that they were simply interested in
gaining "pure" knowledge about Islam and not interested in the sectarian
politics that dominated religious scholarship among other groups. Such a
stance, however, was not categorized as a turn toward Salafi Islam or a
complete rejection of their previous religious affiliation. Although many
women talked about their lives and experiences in terms of how they had
been before they started attending *dars* and after, they did not conceive of
this as a break or complete transformation of their previous lives. Rather,
they predominantly spoke of their commitment as a desire to further
their existing knowledge of Islam, and to build a closer relationship with
Allah. In this regard, their pious commitments were often subsumed
within a broader sense of moving toward a better self over time.

Such a framing contrasts with Schielke's description of the fragmentation of religious lives brought on by the rise of Salafi Islam in Egypt, and
the strict ethical self-cultivation that it promotes.[20] As I describe in the
next section, the women attending *dars* gatherings or a Quran school do
not altogether cease being Hanafi or following their particular *fiqh*.[21]
Family law in Pakistan incorporates *fiqh* into the state's law; marriage,
divorce, and inheritance of property is decided by the school a person
belongs to. Most of the families that I worked with still followed that law

to decide matters of inheritance, distribution of property, or divorce and, on such matters, sought the advice of established orthodox scholars. It was predominantly in matters of everyday life that most women used their knowledge of Quran and Hadis. Of course, this does not mean that the differences between the practices encouraged at *dars* or in Quran schools did not conflict with what they had previously practiced, or were not a source of tension in relation to family expectations, obligations, and other aspirations. However, as I explain, such tensions did not lead to fragmentation, but were rather a source of ongoing negotiation, debate, and deliberation.

The desire to distance oneself from religious politics and tensions at home matches with some of the experiences of the Muslim community in the West. In addition, it reflects some of the broader problems of self-censorship and self-policing that are associated with self-representation in the presence of an (imagined) outsider. The idea of universal or "global" Islam, commonly evoked by diaspora Muslims in the United States and Europe, has often been read as a response to the contested place of Islam in Western societies. Examples from the United States, in particular, suggest that global Islam allows diaspora groups to establish themselves as part of mainstream American society while adhering to an abstract and cosmopolitan Muslim identity.[22] This process often involves silencing voices or eradicating practices that are perceived as an embarrassment within a larger mainstream society. Appealing to a universal and homogenized Islam—"true Islam" as it is often called—allows diaspora groups to distance themselves from the "embarrassing" culturally specific Islam of their parents' home countries. Meanwhile, this "true Islam" often "enshrines values that are consistent with enlightened middle-class American attitude."[23] For instance, Shryock writes that Arab Americans in Detroit prefer a public image that is consistent with mainstream American geopolitical interests and values. Arabs whose views do not match this image, especially on Zionism and U.S.-Israel relations, are discredited as "backward" or as "boaters" (simple migrants) who are not attuned to the universal Islamic values of the real Arab Americans.

Likewise, the attendees of Quran schools and *dars* gatherings in Lahore used their relationship with the text to distinguish themselves from local religious groups. In doing so, they aspired to reach an understanding of

Islam that was "pure" and devoid of any politics and sectarian tensions, much like the "true" Islam of American diaspora Muslims. Moreover, the emphasis on reading, understanding, and conscious reflection—much of which relies on literacy and modern education—in pious middle-class groups reflects anxieties about self-representation, similar to those experienced by diaspora Muslims. In an environment where social hierarchies are inflected with modernist ideals, this emphasis allowed them to showcase their own progression. Through their effort and learning, my informants highlighted that their commitment was not out of ignorance or a sense of "tradition," as stereotypically assumed, but the result of critical reflection and choice. Any voices that ran counter to this image, such as the _khaṭīb_ mentioned earlier, were condemned as "backward." Here, their views are similar to those of American Muslims groups who aim to propagate an "enlightened" image of their community.

In the face of a "global" audience that is perceived as viewing Muslims as "extremists" and as "irrational," most urban Pakistanis—pious or otherwise—argue that religious terrorism and violence is the result of illiteracy, ignorance, and "backwardness." Armbrust has noted a similar pattern in the depiction of Islamists in Egyptian cinema. He illustrates how films that portray Islamists as illiterate or from the upper Egyptian countryside (the stereotypical site of backwardness for Cairo) are more popular among locals when compared to films that show Islamists as educated professionals.[24] While such depictions reveal the self-policing and self-censorship inherent in mass-mediated Muslim self-representation, they are also indicative of an underlying faith in the ideals of teleological progress and modernism, an aspect I return to in the next section.

At _dars_ gatherings in Lahore, the women present often emphasized how this kind of engagement with the Quran helped build a personal relationship with Allah, for it encouraged thinking about Islamic practices in relation to their own lives and experiences. For instance, referring to the common practice in _dars_ of explaining the context in which a verse was revealed, an attendee explained how this helped establish an understanding of the continuing relevance of Islam. She said that in discussing the verse in relation to the context and time in which it was revealed, the attendees were encouraged, in the ensuing discussion and after, to draw linkages with present circumstances. This process allowed them to realize

that Islamic practices are not dictates chained to a specific time or lifestyle, but relevant for all kinds of contexts and circumstances. "Once you
think about it like this . . . [in relation to the] time it was revealed in,
and how it speaks to the time you live in, you see how compatible it is
with modern life."[25] Speaking about her own experiences, she revealed
how this kind of engagement had been central in her decision to start
wearing a *ḥijāb*.

> When Islam is not distinguished from culture, it exists in your thinking
> as linked to it . . . you cannot separate the two. The problem with that is
> that when your culture evolves, you think that now there is no need for
> Islam. So in our minds, purdah is linked to a culture where women are
> made to stay at home—*ćādar ćār dewarī* (confined in four walls and a
> chador). So, when you have moved on from this culture and progressed . . .
> women now are educated, they go out to work . . . then veiling too seems
> outdated . . . what use is it to me, someone who is working [kindergarten
> teacher] outside the home, drives to work. But then, when I read the
> Quran and learnt about the context and reason . . . to mark the difference
> between believing and nonbelieving women . . . what it says on building
> modesty . . . it made me see the relevance of it for my life right now.

This woman's views were shared by others at *dars* gatherings, and it was
common to hear people talking about the importance of reflecting upon
Quranic verses in relation their own lives and needs. It was this kind of
personal engagement, they claimed, that allowed them to see that Islam
was not only compatible with middle-class life but also beneficial in terms
of dealing with the demands it made.

Such ideas on the active pursuit of knowledge and reflection have been
furthered through a flow of return-migrants from the United States.
Return-migrants were a common presence at *dars* gatherings in new
middle-class circles. Often, they were spouses of doctors, while others
were married to computer engineers, software developers, and foreign-
educated university lecturers. Many of them had started attending Islamic
centers and holding religious study circles while living in the United
States. It was through their experiences at the Islamic centers that they
realized how, despite having lived in a Muslim country, they knew very

little about their own religion. Rubina's reflections serve as an illustration of the sense that many expatriate families had of discovering Islam in the United States. She had grown up in Lahore, but moved to the United States soon after marrying a doctor who was finishing his residency in a small town outside of Houston. She explained how "in Pakistan, ... even when I first moved [to Houston], I had never thought of Islam much."[26] However, this changed when her children were born. "In Pakistan, you don't have to think about these things, but in America, you worry how your children will have Muslim values ... so we thought of weekend classes at the Islamic center for them." It was through these visits that Rubina came to understand the importance of acquiring Islamic knowledge. "It was then when I realized how little I knew. I was lucky to be born Muslim, but I had not made an effort to understand my religion." Rubina soon started taking lessons in Quranic exegesis at the center. "What drew me to these lessons was that the focus was on the Quran itself. Our instructor always separated culture from religion ... we just focused on the Quran and learnt how to lead the life that Allah intends for Muslims."

Rubina's experiences and views on Islam in the United States were shared by other expatriate families. And, like Rubina, many of them continued their Islamic learning and started hosting and attending *dars* gatherings in their homes and neighborhoods in Lahore. At these gatherings and through their broader social interactions and linkages, they encouraged other women to study the Quran by presenting them with examples of how Islam was practiced in the United States. In many of the *dars* gatherings that I attended, the *dars*-giver had some experience of living abroad, and would often use examples from her time there while explaining a particular *āyāt*. Even in cases where the *dars*-giver had not spent time outside Pakistan, it was not unusual to find return-migrants in attendance. Their experiences abroad and knowledge of Islamic practices outside Pakistan were often a point of conversation before and after the formal *dars,* when many of the women sat together and chatted. Such connections were actively cultivated and displayed—several times, for instance, I was expressly told by the host to listen to the views of a particular attendee because she had been living in the United States—and served to legitimize the "modern" nature of the gatherings. For many of my informants, who had never traveled abroad themselves, these associations and the flow of information they provided were a way of fostering ties with a larger Muslim community.

At the same time, however, these connections and the broader engagement with "global" Islamic practices were not without tensions and ambiguities. Such instances, however, did not lead to a "fragmentation" of worldviews but, rather, often became sites of ongoing debate and discussion.[27] As mentioned, the separation of Islam from cultural practices, a distinctive feature of "global" Islam, was often locally praised. Distinguishing between the two was viewed as a way of removing "backward" cultural practices that were not consistent with Islamic teaching, as well as with a progressive middle-class lifestyle. Many members of the new middle-class, for instance, claimed that the backward practices of dowry or not allowing women the right of divorce were thought of as Islamic when they were, in fact, cultural practices influenced by Hinduism. They claimed that with the growing emphasis on Islamic learning, Pakistanis were beginning to recognize some of these misconceptions, but they were still much behind Muslims in the West. This meant that it was not always easy to act upon such distinctions between what was Islamic and what was mere culture. Such tensions, between religious prescription and local expectation, often surfaced in moments of stress and in relation to family obligations. Among *dars* circles, local traditions following a death, such as holding a *Quran-Khānī* after forty days (*ćālīsā*) and on death anniversaries were considered as *bid'at*, a deviation from the true teachings of Islam. Following the guidance in Quran and Sunna, they maintained that Islam only allowed three days of mourning and that anything would question the will of Allah. It was, however, not always easy for some to act on these views, since they often felt duty bound to conform to social norms and expectations for the sake of their larger families.

This dilemma became a source of tension for Saima, an acquaintance from one of the *dars* gatherings, when her mother-in-law passed away after a long illness. When I visited her house to condole, along with some other women from *dars*, she mentioned that she was going to hold a *ćālīsā* for her mother-in-law. Saima told me she had initially not wanted to hold one; the guidelines in the Quran were clear that only three days of mourning are prescribed. Both she and her husband were in agreement on this but he was under considerable pressure to hold one out of a sense of obligation to his father and siblings. Saima's parents-in-law had lived with them, so the extended family expected them to host the event in their house. It was a difficult decision for her and one that had been the source of tension, but in the end, she had decided to hold the *ćālīsā*. She told me that it was already such a painful and difficult time for her husband and that she did not want to create further problems for him at this stage. "I did not want to see the brothers fighting amongst themselves or that they accuse my husband of not being a good son," she said.[28]

Saima explained that she had felt conflicted about what her foremost duty was in this instance. On the one hand, she explained, "There are guidelines in the Quran on death rites"; on the other hand, "One has duties as a wife on how to look after your husband and family . . . to keep them happy but also to protect their honor." She continued,

> In an ideal situation, one would not have to choose, but over here when people are so behind in these things, these tensions arise. Besides, you know how people are. I don't want them to think that I am avoiding my responsibilities . . . that I found looking after her for so many years such a chore that now I am so glad to be free that I can't even do this.

In this instance, Saima had decided to put her duties as a wife and daughter-in-law first, although it had meant going against the prescription on the permissible time for mourning. As I was leaving, Saima told me, "Some people [at *dars*] understand that these things are difficult and you make the best possible choice based on your learning and position, but some do not." Referring to particular return-migrants who also attended her *dars*, she said,

> When people have been living abroad for some time, they forget these pressures. Over there, living alone, it is easy to make changes to your life, it is just you. But it is different over here . . . you need to remember the people and environment around you. Sometimes people who have been away too long become hard *(sakht)* and forget these things.

Saima's decision to hold a *ćālīsā* was, indeed, criticized by some attendees of her *dars* gathering, including the return-migrants she had referred to, while others were more supportive of her decision. Rather than outright

condemnation or acceptance—although some did just that—it was a subject of debate and discussion among the women who came to know of her
decision. For instance, after we had left the house, one of the other women
present, Afshan, said that she had stayed silent when Saima had told us of
the *ćālīsā*, but did not agree with her decision. "I can see that she was
under pressure, but it is exactly in these times that we need to remember
Allah and His *hidāyat* (directives)."[29] Sajida, another *dars* attendee, inter-
rupted Afshan here and argued that it was not so simple because of the
repercussions it could have—the potential for the brothers to fight among
themselves and the family to fall apart. Sajida said that in thinking of
these things, Saima was also following in the path of Allah. "Keeping our
family together is also following in Allah's path," she said, "We come to
the Quran to learn the truth, to move away from the *firqa pasandī* (sec-
tarianism) that is destroying our religion. . . . We have to make sure our
decisions don't become the cause for further divisions."[30]

Afshan replied to this intervention by saying that such decisions were
not theirs to make, their duty was to follow the word of Allah and to
encourage others to do the same. "We cannot be the judge of these things,
we can only follow what is written and let others follow our example. . . .
That is how others will know what is right or wrong, we cannot leave
them in ignorance of what is right." Referring to Saima's earlier comment
about what other people would say about her decision, Afshan claimed
that such concerns should not deter them from following the Quran.

> We cannot let this affect us. Of course, it is important to change the
> hearts of others, but by teaching them what is right through our own
> example. There is no need to worry about being judged by others, our
> *a'māl* (deeds) are there for all to see. . . . If they cannot recognize the
> truth in them, we should just keep going on regardless. Allah is our judge.

Afshan and Sajida continued to talk during the journey and their views
generated a larger discussion on the topic among the other women in the
car. By the end of the trip, there was no unanimous decision on what was
the correct course of action in this instance. Neither Afshan nor Sajida
had been convinced by the other's position but their views were indicative of how they understood their commitment, and their duties to

Allah, in relation to the environment around them. As much as "global" Islam—and the global Muslim community it fosters—offers a way to rise above and beyond the local, its methods encourage a way of thinking that brings the local back into focus. By emphasizing the continued relevance of Islam, it opens space for questioning and reasoning in relation to one's own circumstances and position.[31]

At the same time, there was a parallel sense among many at *dars* gatherings that it was not always easy to live up to their pious commitments, and that they had to maintain a careful balance between their goals and other obligations. These tensions were often expressed, as Saima had done, by criticizing the strict expectations of return-migrants, and those who had spent a long time within Islamic communities abroad. Here, people who had been living away from Pakistan were depicted as unable to understand local concerns because they had become too used to living alone, or only among people who shared their views. Often, I heard women at dars gatherings maintain that when one lived abroad, one could choose the people that one interacted with and, in the process, form part of a like-minded community. This, however, was not always possible in Pakistan where one was restricted through various family networks and commitments. Thus, while many spoke admiringly of the effort made by Muslims abroad to lead a pious life, it was also cross-cut with an awareness that they were not always understanding of the difficulties faced by others at home. As with the conversation after the visit to Saima's house, these tensions were never completely resolved but were a source of ongoing debate and deliberation.

These strains were also discussed in relation to generational differences. Marriage prospects of children was a frequent topic of conversation and, in particular, many worried about finding a suitable and equally pious match for their daughters. Women with daughters of marriageable age often complained that their options were limited, for it was hard to find families who were equally well-educated and pious. They felt that families of the socio-economic level they desired for their daughters were often wary of pious girls, and tended to view them as backward or as rigid in their ways. Meanwhile, families that were accepting of their commitment to a religious life were not equally progressive, conflating Islam with the conventional cultural norms of expecting women to be not very interested in education and not wanting them to work. Fatima, an informant from Amina *bājī's dars*, explained the problems she faced when looking for a match for her daughter, Saba, who had done a course from Al-Huda two years prior.

> I used to get worried, thinking how will we find a suitable match for Saba. You know how it is, there is a feeling that if a girl wears a *ḥijāb*, she won't fit in . . . families get very hesitant. We got a good proposal from a well-to-do family with good morals . . . up-bringing . . . and the boy had his MBA and worked in a bank. . . . We liked the family very much. But the boy wanted Saba to not wear a *ḥijāb* and she immediately said no when she heard that. What they were asking for was difficult, not what we believe. But we also knew that it will be hard to find another proposal like this so I asked Saba to reconsider. These decisions are not easy but she was at least willing to consider . . . so many of our girls don't nowadays.[32]

Fatima's experience was indicative of how pious commitments are not always aligned with desires and aspirations for upward mobility. While the cultivation of personal ethics fostered links with an identity and world that extended beyond Pakistan, it sometimes created tensions locally. More importantly, her end remark, about the unwillingness of younger women, reflects a broader anxiety in pious circles. Although young people were frequently commended for the strength of their belief and convictions, there was, at times, a parallel sense that they were becoming too *sakht* and that it made life difficult for them. As Fatima later said, "they [young people] forget sometimes that they need to live in this world, and that it is not perfect". Interestingly such concerns were also articulated by some pious return-migrants, who were otherwise often perceived as being *sakht* themselves. As explained earlier, for most of the return-migrants, being close to elderly parents and familiarizing their children with Pakistan had been the primary motivation for returning. Those who had returned with grown-up sons and daughters sometime expressed concern about their marriage prospects and, more generally, their ability to adapt to life in Pakistan.

One of my informants, Rehana, had returned from the United States with grown-up children. She was proud of her children's commitment to an Islamic life—her son and two daughters had become active in the local

Islamic center in Minneapolis—but often apprehensive about their ability to find suitable matches among Pakistanis. Rehana's family had moved back because of her husband's elderly parents—his father had since passed away—and also to find spouses for their children. Given the economic conditions in Pakistan, her children should eventually go back to United States but wanted them to marry here before they did. "It is always better to get married among your own people," she would say, "and we thought that moving back would give them a greater chance of finding the right person."[33] However, she found that, used to the Muslims and Muslim life of the United States, they often found that the prospective matches they were introduced to here often did not share their attitude toward Islam.

The dilemmas, inconsistencies, and ambiguities in the pursuit of a pious life were frequently viewed as a result of a broader lack of knowledge and commitment in Pakistan. Replicating the modernist trajectory, in which Pakistan was behind and needed to catch up, my informants talked about the difficulties of following "real" Islam in Pakistan in comparison to places—often the West—where there was greater emphasis on learning. Yet equally, underlying these discussions was also a sense that this world was inherently an imperfect place but that it had to be engaged with, something that the ideals of "global" Islam did not always account for. Such ideas were not prevalent among those on the fringes of the movement for a personal understanding of the Quran, but sometimes articulated by those who have initiated it. For instance, one of the older teachers at Al-Huda once told me that she found that, over time, although there was an increase in Islamic knowledge in recent years, it had been accompanied by a lack of sensitivity to the world around us. She said that when they had started Al-Huda, it had been with the intention to impart Islamic knowledge so that people knew what was right and wrong. They wanted women to incorporate Islamic values in their lives without having to rely on another person for guidance. As she put it, "We want women to have a direct relationship *(rishta)* with Allah." However, she added, "Building this *rishta* does not mean you break your previous *rishtas* in the world. You need to take these forward with you . . . *dunyā ke sāth čalnā.*" She went on to say that, in their eagerness to learn and understand the word of Allah, there was a tendency for young women especially to forget this.

CHOICE, AUTHORITY, AND RATIONALITY

In her exegesis at *dars* gatherings and in lectures at Al-Huda, Dr. Farhat Hashmi does not follow any particular school of jurisprudence. She usually makes several references to Maulana Mawdudi but does not exclusively rely on his *tafsīr* and, on many occasions, offers her own opinions. She also frequently quotes the Great Imams but, disregarding the human chains of scholarship in Islamic jurisprudence, does not follow a particular school. Other teachers in the school base their lectures on Dr. Farhat Hashmi's teachings and do not follow the dictates of any one established Muslim scholar. Similarly, at most of the *dars* gatherings that I attended—led by women trained both at Al-Huda and elsewhere—the *dars*-givers did not confine themselves to one school of thought and, instead, gave opinions from a range of jurisprudential scholars. Most of the Quran schools attended by middle-class groups in Lahore usually follow the Al-Huda model and draw upon a wide range of commentaries and opinions. Even the Quran schools that do follow a particular *fiqh* tend to downplay their sectarian associations and, instead, emphasize their commitment to building a personal understanding of the Quran, and of the broader importance of acquiring religious knowledge.

The position that a Muslim has the right to follow any of the imams from the four schools of Islamic jurisprudence has become increasingly common in the twenty-first century and, in particular, has been taken by many of the contemporary female-led piety movements. Saba Mahmood, for instance, has noted a similar freedom in choosing juridical opinions in the women's mosque movement in Cairo.[34] In Arabic, taking such a position is called *talfīq*, but in Lahore the more common term is *gair-muqallid* and is often used pejoratively by orthodox Islamic scholars. The practice is also associated with Salafi Islam. As mentioned earlier, most of the students of Al-Huda, and the women at Quran schools more broadly, did not identify with any of these terms. On the one hand, they maintained that they did not want to be associated with any one sect, and that their position was that "of a Muslim, and nothing else." For them, the freedom to choose an opinion was closely connected to the effort and commitment required to lead a pious life. It was indicative of their familiarity and engagement with the text and of the reflection that had gone into their decisions. In this respect, they contrasted it with a "blind following of tradition" that they believed had become commonplace in Muslim countries, like Pakistan.

On the other hand, this freedom was often not viewed as being Salafi or as a break away from Hanafi Islam, the school of jurisprudence that is most widely followed in Pakistan. When asked directly, few of the families who I interacted with shared an identification with Salafi Islam. Instead, most tended to reemphasize their position as a Muslim and decried the need for any kind of sectarian affiliation, including Salafism. These positions were not viewed as being contradictory, perhaps because they were often exercised in different domains. Family law in Pakistan incorporates *fiqh* into the state's law; marriage, divorce, and inheritance of property are decided by the school a person belongs to. Most women at Al-Huda, and at *dars* gatherings generally, still followed this law on such matters and would seek the advice of established orthodox scholars. The teachers at Al-Huda themselves often called established muftis of Deobandi or Barelwi training to give advice to women on matters such as divorce. Although questions relating to Islamic law were often discussed, it was largely in issues of everyday life and conduct that most women used their knowledge of the Quran and Hadis. Moreover, the women at *dars* gatherings, and the larger families and social circles that they belonged to, had rarely received religious education at an Islamic seminary or traditional institution. Apart from learning to read the Quran in Arabic with a teacher, compulsory Islamic studies in school had been their only formal source of religious learning. In this respect, not only had their sensibility about religion been shaped by mass education, but they had also been exposed to the generic Islam of the state. Like "global" Islam, the "generic" Islam of the state is focused on the universals of religious practice and, in its vision of a unified community, plays down any differences or divisions. The majority of the women at Al-Huda and at *dars* gatherings were critical of the state's education system and its treatment of Islam but, as I elucidated, also echoed its logic in their own practices.

As discussed in the last section, the aim of women at *dars* gatherings was to use their knowledge and learning to incorporate Islamic values and ethics into their daily lives and dealings with others. As one informant once put it, "You want to bring Islam back into your life in a way that it relates to everything that you do."[35] Her comment here reflects the larger sense within these pious circles that Islam was given limited space and largely considered irrelevant in contemporary urban life. Amina *bājī* would often say during her *dars* that "religion has just become *khānā purī*."[36] For instance, in her *dars* on Surat Al-Baqarah [2:1], which touches on issues of debt, usury, and commercial transactions, Amina *bājī* explained the meaning of each āyāt and briefly talked about its contemporary relevance.

> These days, all Islam is about *khānā purī*. A woman prays five times a day or she keeps all her fasts in *Ramazān* and thinks that she has fulfilled her obligations as a Muslim. But Islam is much more than that. It is a complete *way of life* that we need to incorporate into our lives. Like in this Surat, the Quran guides your business dealings. Similarly, there is advice in the Quran and Hadis for all aspects of our life. We cannot say that to live a Muslim life is to say our daily prayers or to fast; it is to include these teachings in all aspects of our lives. Only then will Muslims progress as a nation.[37]

Amina *bājī's* disdain with the compartmentalization of Islam was shared by others. At another *dars* gathering, one attendee mentioned how such sessions had helped her understand the relevance of Islam in her social relationships, particularly when it came to managing time between her obligations with her in-laws compared to those with her parents. The Quran, she told me, has guidelines on how to approach every aspect of our lives but there is little recognition of this in our society. She continued, "Most people's attitude is like what is done in school, [where] you fit everything to do with religion in one subject [Islamic studies], teach it one hour a week, and that is all the relevance it has."[38]

The construction of religion as a distinct category—which can be relegated to particular domains—is a feature of the modern public sphere. In the case of South Asia, such treatment of religion arose out of colonial rule and forms of governmentality, but has largely remained in place in postcolonial Pakistani and how the state handles Islam.[39] My interlocutors were critical of the state's treatment of religion, and of its broader position in the public sphere, yet they replicated much of the same logic.

Although they wanted to disregard the relegation of religion to particular domains, they accomplished this by treating it as a distinct subject that could be studied, understood, and then applied to all aspects of life. Mandana Limbert has noted a similar pattern among women's religious study circles in Oman, which were heavily critical of state schools' handling of Islam but, at the same time, significantly influenced by them. She writes that just as religion was treated as a separate subject in schools, the women in religious study circles saw Islam as a "distinct category of life and one that requires participation."[40] Likewise, the women at *dars* gathering were critical of the way Islamic studies was taught in schools. Many complained that schools did not bother to develop a real understanding of Islam. However, their eagerness to learn and understand the Quran, like any other subject, tended to reinstate the logic of schooling. As Starrett has noted of Islamic studies schoolbooks, which often turn religion into a system of ideas that can be explained, my informants believed that, with the right kind of learning and reflection, Islam could be known and applied in everyday life.[41]

It was not only the underlying sense of religion as a discrete system of ideas that showed the influence of modern schooling, but also the language, discourse, and points of reference through which their choices and actions were explained. As Mahmood has also noted, *talfīq*—that is, the right of choosing a juristic opinion from any school of law—gives precedence to individual judgment and choice, but it treats these notions in a manner different from liberal humanism.[42] It allows an individual to choose an opinion, even if it is a minority one, but the choice is not made on the basis of personal preferences or inclination. Instead, as Mahmood puts it, "The form of reasoning followed in exercising a choice must be guided by the requisite rationale and capacities that jurists deemed authoritative."[43] The procedure is evident in the sermons and lectures by Dr. Farhat Hashmi in which she lists the juristic opinions on a particular issue and then explains why she is choosing a particular one. Yet following this deliberation, she often lends authority to the opinion by explaining it through concepts and ideas borrowed from liberal humanism and discourses on science and rationality. For instance, this is noticeable in her views on veiling, where she follows the mainstream opinion requiring women to veil in the presence of *namehram* and to dress modestly.[44] In order to explain why women are required to veil, she quotes relevant passages from the Quran and Hadis and gives a range of juristic opinions before explaining her own decision. However, she then further justifies her position by talking about the moral and social evils in society and the objectification of women's bodies in the media.

In one of her lectures that I attended at a local library, Dr. Hashmi explained the importance of veiling and gender segregation by discussing the effect of extramarital affairs on children. She maintained that veiling and avoiding contact with *namehram* men helped reduce the chances of such liaisons. She then moved on to discuss the objectification of women in films and advertisements. "Is there any freedom in walking around in a bikini to sell something?" she asked. The audience nodded as she continued, "What freedom is there when your body is used as bait to sell something, when it becomes a way to get male attention? Are you really more free?" Here, her views on veiling followed the mainstream juristic opinions on veiling used by traditional clerics and religious movements, but her explanation also overlapped with, and borrowed from, feminist and anticapitalist critiques of the objectification of women.

Likewise, students at Al-Huda often linked "true" knowledge of Islamic teachings and practices with the teaching tools and methods through which they were taught. For instance, many of them spoke about the use of PowerPoint presentations in the lessons and seminar-style teaching with time for question-and-answer sessions. Moreover, they reminded me that at Al-Huda they were always encouraged to research the topics they were studying, and to rely on multiple references. As one informant put it,

> This is not a joke, you have to work so hard here. And when we have presentations, it's not like we can read from one book and then just repeat it. We are encouraged to do *real research*. We look at different things, go online, and research. It's not just like that.[45]

Many of the students made direct reference to the use of modern teaching tools. For instance, the reliance on audiovisual aids in lessons was often given as evidence of the commitment of Al-Huda to deliver "real" knowledge. In this respect, it appeared that the authority of the institute and the authenticity of its message flowed from the teaching tools and techniques themselves. Although authorial voice and genealogical chains of transmission are central to traditional Islamic pedagogical techniques, there was a striking disregard for such forms of authority here.[46] As much as this shift indicates a sensibility shaped by mass education, it also conveys a wider conviction in the promises and symbols of teleological progress. The idea that the "real" Islam can be found in the text not only relies on education, the bastion of postwar modernism, but also places faith in the methods and technology associated with it.

Outside of Al-Huda, at *dars* gatherings and in discussions in pious middle-class circles, people often drew upon science and rationality when explaining Islamic teachings or the merits of a particular juristic opinion. Here too the dictates and judgments that were favored were often in line with mainstream opinions, but were justified through their compatibility with a rational and scientific worldview. This included, for instance, explaining the requirement of ablution before daily prayers as promoting community hygiene and preventing the spread of diseases or justifying the rules for halal slaughter in terms of the diseases carried in animal blood and the humaneness of the method. My informants often mentioned how many of the directives in the Quran and Hadis were also now advocated by modern science; for example, the ideal time (two years) a mother should breastfeed her child. Such appeals to discourses of science and rationality were complemented with comparisons of Islamic teaching with sociopolitical norms associated with the West. My informants remarked, for instance, that the political system of democracy is usually associated with the West but its principles and ideas had been part of the Prophet's teachings. They maintained that the last sermon given by the Prophet shortly before his death should be considered the first charter of democracy in terms of its emphasis on equal representation, redistribution of wealth, and social justice. Similarly, it was common to hear people talk about the sense of discipline and appreciation for punctuality, essential for modern life, that was inculcated through the five daily prayers.

In highlighting the increased use of discourses of rationality and science in pious circles of the new middle class, my intention is not to suggest that such principles and forms of inquiry are new to Islamic learning. Critique, reason, and rationality have always been a part of debates and contestations in scholarly Islamic discourses.[47] Moreover, the discussions and ideas I have described do not always draw upon the scientific method of inquiry or reasoned critique. Instead, they emphasize the continued relevance of Islamic teachings for contemporary middle-class life by showing its compatibility with a scientific and rational worldview. An appeal to these points of reference is indicative of the larger imagined audience that is being addressed, and where my informants situated themselves in relation to it. At the same time the insistence in pious circles that religion should govern all aspects of everyday middle-class life positions Islam within a broader economy of knowledge, an environment where such religious precepts are discussed in relation to other worldviews and ideologies. Such comparisons and dialogues encouraged generalized rationalization of Islamic teachings and practices, as was evident in the discussions in pious circles on the continued relevance of Islam in modern life.

A parallel can be drawn here with Iqtidar's argument that competition between religious groups can encourage secularization. Focusing on Lahore, she notes that the Islamist groups under her study operate predominantly within the same demographic—lower middle-class and working-class groups—and have to contest among themselves for recruitment and appeal. This competition to win over supporters to their particular concept of a "good Muslim life" leads not only to changes in stances but also to a certain rationalization as groups try to appeal to the larger needs of the demographic. In turn, she argues that the presence of varying models of a "good Muslim life" stimulates debate and rationalization among supporters as they try to choose a group that best suits their needs. It is this rationalization, Iqtidar argues, that can be viewed as provoking broader secularization. In contrast to this, in the pious middle-class circles that I describe, it was not competition between groups as much as comparison with other ideologies and worldviews, alongside broader middle-class aspirations, that fostered generalized rationalization. That said, however, the influence of this form of personalized piety on debate and dialogue in other religious groups was noticeable. As mentioned leaders and followers of traditional religious movements, such as the Tablighi Jamaat, have often denounced Quran schools like Al-Huda for being Wahhabi.[48] Yet in recent years, as female Quran schools have gained prominence, an effort has been made on the part of the Tablighi Jamaat to encourage women to join the movement alongside their brothers and husbands. In many middle-class neighborhoods, female gatherings are now organized alongside the usual weekly meeting *(halqā)* for men. I occasionally attended one of these neighborhood gatherings where I noted a marked attention in discussions on the compatibility of Islam with scientific knowledge and middle-class sensibilities.

This was particularly the case when the speaker at the *halqā* invited women from our meeting to visit and attend her lecture at a local medical college's hostel. Ayesha *bājī,* the speaker, often referenced science in her weekly speech but in one lecture I attended she explained to the audience how numerous discoveries made by modern scientists had been mentioned in the Quran and that many of the precepts in Islam made "scientific sense":

> When we do ablution, we are clean, we get rid of bacteria and germs. Without even realizing, we are being hygienic and clean by following Allah's command to pray: . . . girls, as future doctors you know how bacteria and dust stick to your hair and when you see a patient, you want your hair covered.[49]

Some days later, when Ayesha *bājī* and I met again, I asked her why she had chosen to focus on science and medicine rather than on the "six points" that form the core of the Tablighi Jamaat's mission which are usually at the center of their *bayān* (exposition).[50] She replied to my queries by pointing out the importance of knowing the audience that one is trying to appeal to. "Ammara," she said, "this is not unusual, I speak differently to you than I do to someone who does not have university degrees."[51] Ayesha *bājī* went on to explain that

> when I speak to you, I know your mind works in a different way to other people who are not so *education-minded.* I need to appeal to your brain differently than I would to someone who has not read so much. Our *dīn* (religion) holds answers for all facets of life, we take from it what will appeal to that person, convince them on their terms so that they become keen to learn more. In a medical college, you need to show people Islam understands that side of them, so I talked about that.

Ayesha *bājī's* comments reveal how, in the face of competition from other groups, there is an awareness within the Jamaat of the need to appeal to the lifestyle and sensibilities of an expanding middle class. As I have described, this has resulted in some subtle shifts in the broader discourse of the Jamaat, including greater emphasis on the participation of women and some references to discourses of science and rationality.[52] Yet such shifts, as well as the increasing prominence of personalized piety, cannot be read within a trajectory toward Weberian rationalization of religious practice. As much as the discourse on personalized piety engages with ideas on science and rationality, it also disengages from such themes by appealing to the higher, and unknowable, rationality of Allah. Most of my informants in pious circles would use their study of the Quran to reveal its compatibility with a scientific worldview while, at the same time, maintaining that it was not always possible to understand Allah's rationale. As a participant at *dars* once put it, "We can always try to gain knowledge, to learn *dīn* to understand Allah's reason, and we should, but we will never wholly know. Everything He says, all that happens is His will, what His reason is for something, we can always pray and ask . . . [but] never fully know."[53] The shifts between these different perspectives have has some overlap with Devji's analysis of nineteenth-century Muslim intellectual debate in the Indian subcontinent.[54] In this context, he argues that the unsystematic nature of Islamic modernism allowed it a degree of fluidity, where scholars chose to engage with Western modernity at certain junctures and withdraw at others. The views of my informants reflected a similar engagement and disengagement. In some instances the Quran was rational because it conformed to a scientific worldview; at other times the Quran had a higher rationality and logic that could not always be understood and explained.

In Lahore, piety centered around the text carries its own forms of "enchanted" thinking. Alongside the desire to cultivate ethics through understanding the Quran, there exists a parallel tendency to "overstand" it.[55] In this way of thinking, one depicts Islam as the source of all wisdom, a fount of ideas to grasp and explain subjects that are not necessarily of religious origin. This tendency was not limited to pious circles but was especially noticeable in such spaces. Among the families that I became acquainted with through the Quran school or *dars* gatherings, I regularly heard discussions on the discoveries and current events which had been presumably predicted in the Quran. For instance, it was claimed that the atomic bomb is mentioned in the Quran, and that a specific verse speaks about a man walking on the moon. Some went as far as suggesting that the Quran reveals that a "man with one leg" will wage war against the Muslim world (according to my informants, General Stanley McChrystal, the commander of the U.S. Army forces in Afghanistan at the time, lost a leg in Vietnam). Such views were, of course, not held by all within pious circles and such proclamations were also subjected to derision and jokes. Yet there was considerable discussion on the secrets held within the Quran, and a significant number of people visited predicted websites and exchanged text messages that talked about the scientific discoveries and historical events that the Quran had apparently predicted.

Moreover, television-based Islamic scholars who focused on such topics were frequently watched and discussed. In particular, the lectures of Dr. Zakir Naik, the popular Islamic "televangelist," on the scientific discoveries predicted in the Quran were extremely popular.[56] During one such lecture delivered to the Oxford Union in 2011, in his usual style of providing numerous references, Naik quotes a particular Arabic verse in which a prediction is made and then offers a detailed translation in English.[57] Naik mentions that scientists "found out about the Big Bang forty years ago but the Quran talks about it 1,400 years ago." He then proceeds to quote Sūra Al-'Anbyā' (21:30), translating it as "do not the unbelievers see that the heavens and the earth were joined together and we closed them asunder." Similarly, he argues that although, in 1577, it was Sir Francis Drake who sailed around the world to add further credence to the existence that the earth was round, the Quran was the original source of this knowledge. He quotes Sūra An-Nāzi'āt (79:30) which he translates as "and thereafter we have made the earth egg-shaped." He proceeds to clarify that the Arabic word used for "egg" actually "refers to an ostrich's egg, which is spherical, exactly how our earth is." Throughout the lecture, he gives various other examples of the scientific discoveries mentioned in the Quran.

Alongside the tendency to "overstand," Naik's lectures are often directed to an imagined audience—one that has to be convinced of the superiority of Islam's message and predictions. In the case of his address to the Oxford

Union, the imagined audience was also the real audience. However, this lecture was immensely popular among new middle-class Lahoris, and many of the predictions that he talked of were regularly mentioned and discussed. What made his lectures so appealing for my informants was not only their content but also the way that the arguments were presented. Naik wears a Western-style suit to all his teaching engagements and prefers to speak in English. His authority does not come from any scholarly genealogy or from an Islamic institution. Instead, it derives from his personal study and knowledge of religious texts, including those of other religions, majority Christianity and, not least, through his command of the Bible. In this way, although his audience is majority "local"— in this context, predominantly, Muslim—the frame of reference that he employs speaks to a broader world. For new middle-class Lahoris, his speeches are appealing because they aim to reposition Muslims, like themselves, and the Islamic text on the global stage.

In this chapter, I have used the desire for a personal engagement with the Quran as a site for unraveling the connections between piety and aspirations for modernity. Within English-language media and the established middle class, the growing popularity of Quran schools and *dars* gatherings are viewed as a shift toward Wahhabism exported from Saudi Arabia. Contrary to this kind of representation, I have shown that exposure to discourses of "global" Islam, whether in Quran schools, at dars gatherings, or through relatives living abroad, does not lead to an uncomplicated adoption of new practices and ideas. Rather, it opens space for deliberation and discussion on what should be followed and what should be left behind as one moves toward a more "modern" life. As debated in this chapter, such decisions are made in relation to religious discourses but are often cross-cut with other tensions, such as family expectations and obligations. Examined in this way, the desire for the personal engagement with the Quran, the decisions and tensions it entails, becomes a nodal point for a whole range of issues concerning class mobility, understandings of modernity, the interpenetration of the local and the global, and the status of the personal against the authoritative.

FOUR

Islam and Consumption

IN THE LAST TWO DECADES, Islam has become increasingly noticeable in Pakistani marketplaces and popular culture. Television-based religious scholars and Islamic talk shows dominate the numerous channels available on local cable networks. Mobile phone companies provide their customers with Islamic ringtones and banks offer Islamic financial services. There is a growing industry for *ḥijāb* and *'abāyah* fashions. Islamic storybooks as well as video and board games for children are also readily available in local markets. To cater to these demands, "Islamic shops" that sell a variety of such goods have proliferated in the popular marketplaces and bazaars of Lahore. These trends in the sale, purchase, and advertising of such goods and services show that Muslims in Pakistan are increasingly consuming the same goods as Muslims in other parts of the world, especially in the West. Advertisements on television and billboards in the city propagate the image of "global Muslims"; a representation of subjects believing in the same principles of Islam and consuming the same goods. Lahoris themselves paint a similar picture; for instance, men and women buying Quran stories for their children are quick to point out that their cousins and relatives in the United States read the same books with their children.

This chapter examines the prevailing trends in religious consumption in Lahore, and in urban Pakistan more broadly. Such an inquiry will help in analyzing how the new middle class uses religious consumption to assert its own modernness. Moreover, it will allow for a final discussion on the nature of the playing field of modernity in Pakistan.

RELIGIOUS CONSUMPTION AND MUSLIM SUBJECTIVITY

Within an Islamic context, Starrett has defined religious commodities as items "that either have a direct association with acts of worship, as with prayer beads, or, more commonly, bear sacred images or writing, often with only the single word 'Allah' or 'Muhammad'."[1] This includes a variety of items, ranging from prayer mats, headscarves, and 'abāyahs to posters, bumper stickers, key chains, wall hangings, and decoration pieces that display Quranic verses, names of Allah, or pictures and illustrations of Muslim holy places. However, recent literature on Islamic consumption, and examples from the Muslim world, reveal a far wider range of goods that are considered religious but are not directly linked to any form of worship.[2] The use of Islamic video and board games, storybooks, and Islamic dolls for children, Islamic ringtones for mobile phones in Pakistan, and the growing "Christmasization" of *Ramazān* are all examples of a form of consumption that may be centered around religion but often transcends it.[3]

Contemporary scholarship on religious consumption also illustrates the increasing use of Islamic goods in displaying and fostering a Muslim identity. Using religious consumption to create a "Muslim lifestyle" was first noticed among Muslims in the West. In the context of the United States in the early 1990s, Sanyal argues that Islamic organizations sought ways to make Islam appear as an "attractive alternative" to a younger generation captivated by American culture.[4] They did this through summer retreats, youth camps, and media programs. This was also the time that Islamic fashion and Muslim lifestyle magazines began to be published for diaspora Muslims.[5] For instance, the popularity of the Islamic Barbie, Noorat, among Muslims in the West, and the use of Islamic goods to set apart a Muslim house from a non-Muslim one demonstrate the use of consumption in the construction of a Muslim identity and in resisting

foreign cultural influences.[6] In the last decade, the use of religious consumption in making and articulating a particular subject-position has
become popular in Muslim majority areas as well. Carla Jones's work on
pious consumption in Indonesia and Meneley's account of Islamist
Barbies in Yemen reveal the use of religious goods in articulating and
negotiating local class and religious tensions.[7] Elsewhere, Johan Fischer's
illustration of the boycott of American goods in Malaysia after the 9/11
attacks suggests that consumption is not only used for articulating one's
position in a local setting, but can also work as a form of activism against
Western dominance.[8]

In Pakistan too, religious consumption is increasingly employed to
construct a Muslim lifestyle. A majority of such goods have little religious
significance other than the word "Islam" or "Muslim" appearing on them,
although, as I shall discuss shortly, some are consumed precisely because
they help the person better understand Islam. For instance, a growing
number of middle-class women who wear a *hijāb* have started using a
shampoo produced by a well-known multinational company that is especially designed for covered hair. Many such women admit that the
shampoo is not markedly different from ordinary shampoos, but they
derive a sense of satisfaction from it being designed just for them. As one
informant put it,

> Yes, I know that, at the end of the day, it's a shampoo like all others ... but
> this is the only shampoo designed for Muslim women. We always
> use things designed for other people, why not use something that is
> just for us?[9]

Similarly, people who use Islamic debit cards, such as the "*ṣādiq* card"
offered by a local bank, are often aware that the card is no different from
other debit cards but they prefer to use it as an expression of their Muslim
identity.[10]

In recent years, Islamic mobile services have also become popular in
urban Pakistan. These include subscriptions for text messages informing
customers of prayer timings as well as a "Hadith of the Day" and "Ayat of
the Day" service where a verse and its translation are sent to sub-
scribers. However, the most popular service centers on is Islamic

ringtones—Quranic recitations or religious songs (ranging from *qawwālī* to *ḥamd*)—that can be used as sound alerts for an incoming call or tracks to be listened to. Striking here is the large variety of songs that are classified as "religious" by the mobile phone companies. Religious ringtones vary from Quranic verses to *qawwālīs* in the Sufi canon to traditional Urdu and Punjabi *ḥamds* and *na'ats*.[11] English songs by "Islamic" pop singers, such as Yusuf Sami, are also downloaded.[12] In discussions on Islam, there are usually differing views on whether *qawwālīs* can be considered as an expression of devotion. Similarly, some argue that singing *na'ats* in praise of the Prophet is akin to exalting him to the status of Allah. In sum, there is usually little agreement on what constitutes a religious song. Yet I rarely heard anyone complaining about the "religious songs" category used by mobile service providers. Even those who otherwise argue that *qawwālīs* are not Islamic usually do not criticize their use as Islamic ringtones. "That's just an expression of our identity as Muslims," was a response I often encountered when I asked about the inclusion of such songs. It appeared that when constructing a "Muslim identity" for display to the outside world, personal differences about what constitutes Islamic disappear. Most people in Lahore see Islamic ringtones as an expression of their identity and a display of their individual taste. As one informant put it, "My ringtone reflects my identity as a Muslim but it is also about my personal choice. . . . I use a tune that really expresses me as well."[13]

Religious consumption may suggest greater individual autonomy in the sense that it provides people with an avenue to display their identity. Yet, at the same time, it has emerged in a socioeconomic and political context that often limits the spaces available for individual expression. The ever-growing presence of the market has dovetailed with not just a rollback of the state, but also with a narrowing of political alternatives. Earlier work on political Islam in the Middle East in the 1990s contended that Islamism emerged as a response to dictatorial regimes that banned and suppressed any form of political dissent and opposition.[14] In such a context, religion became a way to oppose the state, and the West (particularly the United States) for supporting these regimes. The rise in religious consumption suggests that, increasingly, this form of opposition has become market-based, expressed through personal tastes rather than public activism. In other words, religious consumption across the Muslim world (but certainly not limited to it) is symptomatic of a "privatization of politics," a consequence of the dominance of neoliberal values.[15]

A rise in religious consumption in urban Pakistan could not have been possible without economic liberalization. In the mid-1990s, Pakistan's economy—like the economies of other developing countries—went through a series of "structural adjustments" and reforms that included increased privatization and market expansion. Local private and multinational enterprises were allowed to enter the market, leading to an influx of foreign brand names and mass advertising campaigns. In 2000, the Pakistani state relaxed its controls on the media and started issuing licenses for private television and radio channels, and local business people were able to enter the media market to launch entertainment and news channels.[16] These channels, along with other popular foreign networks, spurred the growth of the local advertising and marketing industry by providing greater airtime capacity.

Increased consumerism, along with a relaxation on trade controls, has made it a conducive environment for small businesses, such as the Islamic shops that I will turn to below. Moreover, Islamic goods often serve as a form of product expansion for competing private and multinational companies. This is particularly the case with Islamic banking services that have recently gained momentum in the country. From the mid-1990s, international banks, typically headquartered in the West, were the first to offer credit and debit card facilities to the Pakistani public, although these services were usually confined to the very affluent who could afford to pay the minimum deposit needed to open a bank account. In recent years, however, various Gulf-based banks have opened branches in Pakistan, and local banks have also expanded their banking services. Islamic banking, in this context, allows Gulf-based and local banks to offer a differentiated product to customers. In personal interviews, a majority of senior bankers admitted that, in actual practice, Islamic banking does not differ from regular banking, but it appeals to the Muslim sentiments of their customers.

The idea of Muslim conglomerates that challenge the dominance of the West is, indeed, an attractive prospect for most Lahoris, especially at times of heightened tensions with the United States. In the months following the 9/11 attacks, as a consequence of the rise of Islamophobia in the United States, many Pakistanis vowed to never drink Coca-Cola, which they saw as a quintessential symbol of American culture. Instead, they turned to a similar locally produced soft drink, Mecca-Cola, which appeared in the market a few weeks after the 9/11 attacks.[17] Such boycotts are not limited to American products; heightened tensions with India often lead people to temporarily stop watching Indian films and television channels, which are otherwise quite popular in Pakistan. In Lahore, I found that discussions about using consumption (or lack thereof) to challenge the West often led people to recall the oil embargo of 1973. Many would claim that if only Muslim nations could unite to boycott American goods, as they had during the oil crisis, then the U.S. economy would tumble and no longer be a dominant force in the world.

Although drinking Mecca-Cola, or using other "Islamic" products instead of Western ones, is a form of opposition, this method of resisting depictions of Western imperialism is one that reinstates the West at the same time as it attacks it. In this respect, Yaqin writes that Muslims are increasingly relying on a culture of "commodification to recreate their own subjectivity but in doing so, they remain tied down to a culture of consumerism that creates new subjects but still transports them the value of an American lifestyle."[18] As already mentioned, the growing popularity of Islamic Barbies, children's literature on Muslim heroes, and the use of Islamic videogames are all instances where the influence of the West is countered using the very methods by which it is propagated. Toward the end of this chapter, I will return to this theme to discuss the larger consequences of such forms of resistance.

There is, of course, little doubt that the expansion of the market and the consequent rise in consumerism have created an ideal environment for religious consumption. Nor is it false to suggest that neoliberalism, as a larger political project that has elevated the moral primacy of the individual, has changed the nature and scope of politics, including transforming the relations between states and citizens. Yet to take market expansion as both the starting and end points on such arguments—as the contemporary left is frequently susceptible to—does not give us a full picture. For instance, this explanation does not tell us why certain religious goods are more popular than others. Bourdieu reminds us that the construction of taste and aesthetics is not only linked to income levels and economic opportunity. Instead, as Swartz has put it in his reading of Bourdieu, tastes are relational and "preferences express systematic opposition to those of other classes."[19] As illustrated in previous chapters, new middle-class religiosity in Lahore has emerged against a backdrop of opposition to the moral and economic domination of the *khāndānī* and established groups. In this context, new middle-class groups do not use religious consumption simply as an articulation of their (generalized) Muslim identity, but rather to display a particular Muslim subject-position, one that challenges the domination of opposing groups. My ethnography in previous chapters has also shown how such contestations draw upon claims of modernity; the established affluent groups use their modernity to justify their dominant position in society, and, in return, the emerging middle class counters this by depicting themselves and their religiosity as modern and rational. Analyzing the trends in religious consumption thus allows us to see the role that such tensions and competing claims of modernity play in the construction of middle-class tastes.

Wacquant notes that there is a tendency in the social sciences—and this particularly holds true for the literature on consumption—to use neoliberalism as an explanation for the contemporary state of affairs but without explaining exactly how it operates within particular contexts, and often without demonstrating "what is neo about neoliberalism."[20] To imply that neoliberalism carries the same meaning throughout the world, or has the same effects, translates into the assumption that liberalism has also meant the same thing. Uday Singh Mehta's historical research highlights that while nineteenth-century British liberal thought became a foundation for equality in Britain, its emphasis on reason became a justification for the subjugation of the Indian population. Similar justifications, as we have seen in earlier discussions in Chapters 1 and 2, are used by the established groups in urban Pakistan.

ISLAMIC SHOPS AND SHRINES

In Lahore, as in other cities in the Muslim world, shrines have been the typical site for the consumption of handcrafted religious goods, such as *tāwīzs* (amulets), prayer caps, rosaries, cards, and posters with Quranic verses inscribed on them. A stroll down the walled city in Lahore—home to most of the city's Sufi shrines, the traditional sites for religious consumption—will bring you into the presence of *tāwīz* makers willing to make an amulet that will cure illness, resolve family disputes, or keep you safe from the evil eye of your neighbors. Shops across Data Saab, the shrine of eleventh-century Persian Sufi saint Ali Hajvairy, sell posters and key chains bearing Quranic verses or an image of the Prophet's mosque in Medina, along with ceramic models of Mecca, Data Saab, and other famous Sufi shrines. Calligraphers can inscribe verses from the Quran on small cards to hang from the rearview mirror of a car. Parrot fortune-tellers, where the bird picks an envelope bearing a Quranic *āyāt* that holds the key to your future, sit on roadsides.[21] These goods and services are often sold alongside nonreligious ones. The same shops that sell Quranic posters, cassettes, and CDs of religious sermons are also likely to sell posters of Bollywood and Hollywood film stars, soundtracks of Bollywood films, jewelry, perfumes, and plastic toys.

In newer parts of the city, however, Islamic shops have popped up in shopping plazas and markets that only sell Islamic goods. Although each shop may have a different name, such as Al-Balgh Store, Islamic Trends, or Al-Ḥijāb, people in Lahore refer to them generically as "Islamic shops." Such outlets sell headscarves and *'abāyahs;* Islamic video/board games and storybooks for children; Quranic translations and *tafsīrs* (commentaries); books on Islam and Islamic history, and DVDs and CDs of Islamic sermons. I have also seen shops that sold dates and bottled *āb-e-zam zam* imported from Saudi Arabia.[22] Some Islamic shops specialize in a few goods, such as veils and *'abāyahs,* or only Islamic books, while others are more general, carrying an assortment of Islamic goods. Some shops also sell DVDs of films from the Muslim world that, although not Islamic per se, are important for the construction of a broader Muslim identity. I will return to this point below. The distinctive feature of goods in Islamic shops is that they are usually mass-produced and sourced from a variety of foreign countries.

Islamic shops are located in different parts of the city, including the middle-income areas in the southwest of the city and the more affluent areas of DHA. Most shopping malls in the commercial area of Gulberg also host Islamic shops. In more affluent areas of Lahore, designer *ḥijāb*

shops that sell exclusive handmade veils have opened in malls alongside
other foreign and local fashion brands. Islamic shops in less affluent areas
carry cheaper options; they stock *ḥijābs* made by local companies but
often carry some moderately expensive veils imported from the Gulf as
well. Quran storybooks are sold in all Islamic shops as are CDs and
DVDs of Islamic sermons. The main difference between the shops in
affluent areas and those in poorer neighborhoods is the price differential,
as the goods are usually the same.

Shopkeepers at Islamic shops are keen to point out that their businesses differ from the ones found near shrines in the walled city. In a shop
called Islamic Trends in a small marketplace, I noticed that the decoration
pieces on display—small bowls with Quranic verses written inside—were
of a similar type to those sold in the walled city. I mentioned this to the
shopkeeper and he hastily replied:

> They are not the same ... maybe they look like the ones you have seen
> there [at shrines] but these are different. The most important thing is that
> we aren't like those *quacks* at shrines who tell you to drink out of a bowl
> so that you are miraculously healed of your illness. Our bowls are just
> decoration pieces for a Muslim household.[23]

The "*quacks*" that the shopkeeper was referring to are the faith healers
who operate from roadsides or small booths outside shrines. Like the
amulet makers, they often ask their customers to wear an amulet with a
particular Quranic verse it in or, if wishing to relieve illness, drink water
from a bowl with a verse inscribed on it. The shopkeeper at Islamic Trends
wanted to distance himself from such practices and made it clear that he
saw the bowl as simply decorative. In various other stores, shop owners
and shopkeepers differentiated their outlets from those found near the
shrine. As one shop owner explained,

> Why should we keep *illogical* and *superstitious* things here? We are a
> modern shop, educated people come to buy things here. We have books
> for people so that they can learn about Islam ... this is not a place for
> blind followers of Islam.[24]

As at Islamic Trends, the owner here was clear about the customers that his shop attracted. People who liked to read and learn about Islam would come to his shop. People who wanted *tāwīzs*, who did not know or read about Islam, were seen as blindly following customs and rituals.

The majority of the customers at Islamic shops come from new middle-class backgrounds. The more expensive "designer" shops usually attract more affluent families from this class. Pakistanis who live abroad, but visit frequently, also peruse such shops to buy *'abāyahs* or Islamic decoration pieces to take back. Customers from middle-income areas of the city's southwest also visit such shops occasionally, either to window-shop or to make a purchase to include in a daughter's dowry or for a special occasion such as a family wedding. A parallel can be made here with Khosravi's work on Tehrani youth who often spend their free time in expensive malls that host shops selling Western wear.[25] Although they can rarely afford such expensive clothes, and indeed have few opportunities to wear them in public, they nonetheless like to view such items in shop windows. Khosravi writes that such practices are not only a means of defying the Islamist agenda of the state but also indicative of the larger aspirations of Iran's urban youth. Similarly, visiting expensive Islamic shops is indicative of the aspirations of material progress felt by the upwardly mobile groups. Some of my acquaintances admitted that they often visit such shops to see the latest trends and then make cheaper imitations for themselves.

Islamic shops also provide a way for new middle-class groups to challenge the stereotypes of being "backward" and to assert their own modernity. A young couple buying Islamic books at a shop of this kind explained their choices the following way:

> [Islamic story books are] able to make children see the truth in Islam.... It's the modern way of learning about religion. We are not "backward" people, our children go to good schools. We want them to read and learn about Islam, about the many truths that exist in our religion.[26]

Like the shopkeepers quoted above, discussions on the quality of goods at Islamic shops inevitably led to comments on the "backwardness" of the forms of consumption associated with shrines. In a later part of our discussion, the same couple expressed a dislike for amulets and the *pīrs* found at shrines. When I asked the husband to explain why he found them distasteful, he replied, "Those are things of the past, of a time when we did not know better." Many people made references to a dark and ignorant past when talking about the belief in amulets. Preferences for the goods in Islamic shops, on the other hand, were often expressed as "these goods make sense" or that "we use them for real reasons, not because of a *backward* belief." Religious consumption here was used not just to display a Muslim identity but, rather, a specific kind of Muslim identity. The buyers and sellers at Islamic shops did not want to be associated with what they saw as "backward" religious goods. Instead, they preferred goods that would show that they are educated and, because of that, modern.

While there is a tendency in new middle-class groups to distance themselves from popular Sufi practices, those belonging to established families tend to do the opposite. Such groups are consumers of goods and services that express their "mystical" outlook. Other than attending *qawwālī* concerts, there is a growing trend among *khāndānī* groups to visit shrines for "cultural" rather than religious reasons. They do not visit old shrines in and around Lahore to pray, although some might, but rather to admire the site's "traditional" architecture and ambience and, more commonly, to attend musical gatherings. Other than the annual *'urs*, a celebration on the death anniversary of a saint, most shrines also host a smaller *'urs* every Thursday, as the eve before Friday is considered to be auspicious in Sufi tradition. Weekly *'urs* usually include a small *qawwālī* gathering or *ḍhol* music. In the last decade in Lahore, going to listen to music at the weekly *'urs* has become a common pastime for the established classes. In particular, before it was closed down, many would go to the shrine of Baba Shah Jamal to listen to the *ḍhol* of a local devotee called *Pappū Sā'īn*.

The shrine of Shah Jamal is located in the southwest of the city, in an old neighborhood that once housed established groups but is now predominantly occupied by new middle-class and upwardly mobile families. *Pappū Sā'īn's ḍhol* performances have been popular among Lahore's working-class population for many decades, but since the early 2000s they became popular among the affluent as well—so much so that he also began to perform in a local Sufi rock band composed of young musicians belonging to *khāndānī* families. Meanwhile, residents of the area find his performances disruptive and un-Islamic. They complain that the Thursday *'urs* attract all kinds of vagrants and that drugs are openly sold at the site. Indeed, when I visited the shrine on a Thursday evening in 2009, the air was thick with the smell of marijuana. In 2012, such complaints by the local residents forced the authorities to ban *Pappū Sā'in's ḍhol* performances. In established circles, this move created much anger and derision, and was, predictably, seen as yet another sign of growing Wahhabism in Pakistan.

For many old-money and established groups, consuming the "traditional" ambience of Sufi shrines is a way of attaching themselves to the local history and heritage of Lahore. The trend to embrace "old" Lahore has led to a revival of ethnic furniture, clothes, and shoes—sold, of course, in expensive stores in shopping malls and commercial areas—as well as to the emergence of rooftop restaurants in the walled city. Offering traditional Lahori cuisine, such cafes are often located along the Mughal-built *bādshāhi* mosque in the walled city. Ironically, though perhaps to be expected, the old-money groups of Lahore have established their dominance through their modernity, specifically the familiarity with, and connections to, the West that their wealth and education provided. Yet now such groups consume the "local" and traditional as an expression of their identity. Meanwhile, the new middle-class uses religious consumption to build and articulate connections with the outside world. I will now turn to discuss this theme through a focus on prevailing *'abāyah* and *ḥijābs*.

VEILING FASHIONS AND ISLAMIC CHILDREN'S LITERATURE

Hijab & Jilbab *(Ḥijāb & Jalbāb)* is an Islamic shop that specializes in headscarves and *'abāyahs*. Located in a shopping mall in Lahore that hosts Western brands and high-end Pakistani designers, Hijab & Jilbab sells handmade *ḥijābs* and *'abāyahs* in colorful silk and cotton styles, geared for middle-class as well as high-end markets. The garments are exclusively designed by the proprietor of the shop, Chanda Chugtai, a housewife who started the business a few years after she began wearing a veil herself. She decided to open the shop to offer women a way of covering themselves without compromising on fashion and hoped that it would encourage more veiling in society. Mrs. Chugtai was worried about "where society was heading" and thought that turning back to Islam would solve contemporary societal problems.

> Look at the number of extramarital affairs in our society, so many women turn away from their families, just like the women they see in soap operas on television. Men don't seem to care either . . . they have no self-control. I thought that offering fashionable veils will encourage women to cover themselves and be modest. Even if, in the beginning, it is not for the sake of religion but only for fashion . . . even then it is beneficial because at least it would prevent men and women from eyeing each other all the time. . . . Our children have mobile phones now, and they are on the Internet, they could be in the same room as you and you have no control on who they are talking to, what is being said. In this time, Islam can help us all; it can create a protective blanket and save people from vulgarity.[27]

Chanda Chugtai, much like others in upwardly-mobile circles, did not view technological advancement as negative but she was concerned about its moral repercussions for society. Similar to the Pakistani state, she felt that Islam could be "put to work" to solve problems, in this case, the perceived vulgarity of sections of society. The desire to "help" society is a common reason given by Islamic shop owners based in affluent areas of Lahore. For instance, Qasim Ali has opened a shop called Islamic Path in the Circular Market, the main commercial area of the affluent DHA, in the hope that it will increase curiosity about Islam among people.

In both these cases, the decision to open an Islamic shop was influenced by the experiences of Muslims in the West. Qasim is a British Pakistani who grew up near Manchester. As a young teenager, his parents regularly sent him to the local Islamic center for Islam and Quran lessons. In his late twenties, he moved to Pakistan and was astonished at how parents did not make an effort to ensure that their children were aware of their religious duties. "They just expect children to learn from their *nāna nāni* (grandparents)," he said, referring to the common practice in Pakistan of parents leaving elders of the family responsible for their children's religious education.[28] "They never read books on Islam or Islamic history, just heard stories from their grandparents." Qasim saw many problems in

Pakistani society—corruption, nepotism, and immorality—that he thought could be solved if people knew more about their religion. Despite his full-time job as an engineer with a cellular network provider, he opened the shop to encourage people to learn more about religion. He now sells different Islamic goods, including a wide array of Islamic books, especially for children, in the hope of getting them interested in Islamic history and how to live a pious life.

The functional use of Islam was obvious in Qasim's desire to open an Islamic shop. Moreover, his experience as a Muslim in the West had shaped his views on religious education in Pakistan. He favors formal religious teaching, through the use of books and lessons, over the informal manner in which children in Pakistan are usually taught.[29] He believes that formalized religious teaching leads to greater understanding of, and interest in, religious issues. By popularizing religious books, he hopes to create a society where people are able to use their religious knowledge to solve social problems such as corruption.

Chanda's decision to veil and to open an Islamic shop was influenced by Muslims living in the West as well. She started to wear a veil in 2006 after her sister, Zainab, convinced her that this was the right path. Zainab had started covering three years earlier, after attending *dars* gatherings in her neighborhood.

> My sister had always been more religious than me. I would just do what my parents told me to do but she was different . . . would always make an effort to read and understand Islam for herself. A Pakistani-American family moved into their neighborhood [in Rawalpindi], they were true Muslims. . . . Even in America, the wife used to have a *dars* for all the Muslim women in the area . . . and she continued the practice here. . . . It was good to have sessions where you read and understand Islam. In the West, they really try to understand things. My sister started going there regularly and started learning about Islam.[30]

As discussed in Chapter 3, Zainab's story of turning to religion through neighborhood *dars* sessions is a common one in new middle-class circles. As mentioned in the discussions concerning Quran schools, *dars* has been popularized in urban Pakistan by returning expatriates. Chanda's account of her sister's transformation also shows that she believed that American Muslims make more effort than Pakistanis to understand the Quran and that it makes the former, in turn, "true Muslims."

There were other ways in which the West influenced Chanda's work. In Pakistan, the traditional style of veiling consists of wearing a *burqā*, a two-piece garment usually made out of black cloth. One part of the *burqā* was a loose, shapeless cloak meant to be worn over one's clothes. The second part consisted of headgear that cover a woman's hair with an attached piece of cloth that could be used to cover the face or be thrown back when not necessary. Another common form of veiling is wearing an *Afghān burqā*, also referred to as a *shuttlecock burqā*, which is a one-piece garment with a stiff round headpiece and a loose cloak attached to it. Like other Islamic shops, Chanda's shop carried neither of these styles. Instead it stocked colorful headscarves that could be worn in a variety of ways and *ʿabāyahs*—some loose, some fitted—in different designs sent by her relatives in Canada. Before she had started veiling herself, her cousins in Canada—her uncle's daughters, who had started veiling after moving abroad—would ask her to make and send *ʿabāyahs* to them. "They would send me the designs they wanted, and then I would get the fabric, explain to the tailor what to make, and send it to Canada when done." Initially, Chanda only made them for her cousins, but later started sending them in bulk to be sold at exhibitions in the Islamic center. Her cousins would send her samples or descriptions of popular designs, before getting them stitched and mailed back.

Television was another source of inspiration for Chugtai. She particularly liked the *hijābs* worn by the presenters on an Islamic call-in show aired on the ARY channel. The ARY channel is part of the ARY Group of Companies, a Dubai-based holding company started by Pakistani businessman Haji Abdul Razzaq Yaqoob. The channel was first launched for Pakistani Muslims settled in Britain but, after 2000, was also aired in Pakistan after the government allowed private media networks to enter the market. The channel predominantly still caters to Pakistani Muslims abroad. The call-in show that Chugtai mentioned had a female host who is based in the Gulf. Her *hijāb*, as the advertisement at the end of the programmed displayed, was made by Al-Hijab-un-Nisa, an online headscarves and *ʿabāyah* company catering to British Muslims.

The different influences in the headscarves sold at Hijab & Jilbab take us from Lahore to Toronto to Dubai. In Chanda's story, we find a recurring interest in what Muslims in the West are doing. Yet, at the same time, there is a certain arbitrariness in the processes at work. While Mrs. Chugtai was at times consciously imitating her Muslim cousins living in Toronto, at other times these links with diaspora Muslims were unconsciously made. These connections and influences are similar to Tarlo's description of *ḥijāb* fashion and trends among Muslim women in Britain, in which she argues that trends in veiling fashions are set through an interaction of different and often removed actors.[31] Moreover, Tarlo argues that the producers and consumers of Islamic symbols and fashions do not reside in the same space. In the case of religious consumption in Lahore, this separation of the producers and consumers of Islamic fashion was obvious—the trends were set by Muslims abroad and consumed by Muslims at home. Even the name of Mrs. Chugtai's shop is an illustration of the flow of information and goods across different countries that set the trends for religious consumption in Lahore. She kept the name Hijab & Jilbab because it reflected the purpose of the store but was also, as she remarked, "a trendy but traditional name." She explained that the word "jilbab" *(jalbāb)* was used in the Quran in reference to veiling; the term was symbolic of Allah's command and therefore traditional. At the same time, it was different from the usual Urdu words for veiling, such as *parda*.[32] Although it was never explicitly said, using "jilbab" also helped in escaping from connotations of "backwardness" implicit in most Urdu words for veiling. The word *jalbāb*, however, is not directly referenced in the Quran, nor is it an Arabic word as most assume. The word *jalabīb* is mentioned in reference to covering oneself in Sūra Al-'Aĥzāb (33:59) and most assume that *jalbāb* is the singular form of the word in Arabic. In fact, the word was first used in the 1980s by British Muslims who wanted a term for veiling that was not parochial; they wanted to distance themselves from the "traditional" Islam of their parents' home countries and to align themselves with a deterritorialized universal Islam. Thus, what Mrs. Chugtai considered as a traditional Arabic term was actually invented and popularized two decades ago by British Muslims.

The popularity of *ḥijāb* and *'abāyah* designs originating from diaspora Muslims is reflective of the local class tensions, I have discussed in earlier chapters, but also of the broader "global stage" in which middle-class groups positions themselves on. When I asked Mrs. Chugtai why she thought that imported *ḥijāb* and *'abāyah* designs were more in demand than local ones, she replied that "they are more convenient" and that such items did not slip off your head like a regular *ḍupaṭṭā*.[33] Later, however, she added that besides the issue of convenience, these new styles were more fashionable and made her feel part of a community.

> When I started to cover myself, I thought I should veil in the same style as my cousins. Just because I was going to wear a veil did not mean I could not be fashionable. Muslims worldwide have different styles and designs ... my cousins would send me such nice designs, they would look good ... and in Canada they know so many Muslims, all from different countries. It made me happy to think I am doing what Muslims all over the world are doing.

At the same time as making one feel part of a "global community," new styles in veiling help in challenging local stereotypes. A few weeks after the conversation noted above, Mrs. Chugtai and I met again. She told me about some customers who had come in with their own *'abāyah* designs that were copied from the well-known veil fashion blog from Britain Ammara Hijabi (http://www.ammarahijabi.blogspot.com). Talking about her customers' insistence that the *ḥijābs* should look exactly like those on the blog, Mrs. Chugtai commented:

> Sometimes I think that people wear the new style because they do not want to be seen as *paindū*.[34] They want to show the world that they are not "backward"... they are not uneducated but that they know their duties and they can fulfill them. You can be fashionable and still cover yourself.[35]

Another informant Amina, who is a housewife in her late forties, confided that when she had first started covering her hair almost a decade ago, she used to feel embarrassed when she bumped into her old school and college friends in the market. During this time, she explained that most women—irrespective of their socioeconomic status—would veil by wearing a *ḍupaṭṭā* over their hair or with a *burqā*. Whenever her friends from college would see her with a *ḍupaṭṭā* over her head—the majority of them did not veil themselves—they would judge her for dressing like an "uneducated person." The implication here was, of course, that veiling was viewed as a retrograde sign. By contrast, Amina felt that more people now veiled, remarking that it was not as difficult as it used to be and that there were more available styles. She now wore a *ḥijāb* and *'abāyah* that she had designed herself that not only expressed her taste but also carried no negative connotations.

For women such as Amina, wearing the new styles in headscarves is a way to show that they are veiling by choice, derived from their knowledge and understanding, and not due to a presumed dated family custom. Ayesha, a college student in her early twenties, said,

> I wear the kind of headscarf I want to. I don't cover myself because my mother veils and I feel that I have to follow her. It is my choice to veil, and I have read and understood why I need to do this myself. I did not have to wear a *burqā* because it was customary in our household. I wore one out of my own will.[36]

In another shop, a couple in their early thirties were choosing *'abāyahs* in different designs. The husband, who had recently traveled to Dubai, was keen for his wife to try the new fashions available. He kept looking at the different styles, pointing out that the ones he had seen women in Dubai wearing.

> You should also wear one [*'abāyah*] like this. I saw so many women wearing them in Dubai. They wore them and went about their life in a normal way—did their shopping, watched films. It was not like they were confined to the house because they veil. This is how it is when you use your intelligence and understand religion. Then you know what you can do and cannot do. You do not have to be a slave to tradition.[37]

Elsewhere, the popularity of children's Islamic literature was also determined by what was perceived to be popular in the United States and Britain. Islamic literature for children in Islamic shops usually comprises books on the Prophet's life or a particular teaching of Islam. The books are filled with colorful illustrations and drawings, using a story format to narrate the teachings of the Quran or an incident from the Prophet's life. According to one shop salesman, the most popular books are part of a series titled *Quran Stories for Little Hearts* and *Prophet Muhammad for Little Hearts*. The book series is published by Good Word Books, an Islamic publishing house that specializes in Islamic books for children and young adults. Launched by Maulana Saniyasnain, the son of well-known Indian Islamic scholar Maulana Wahid-ud-din Khan, the company is based in Delhi but caters mostly to Muslims in the United States. The website also states that Maulana Saniyasnain's children books are referred to as the "Harry Potter Books of Islam" and are the most popular Islamic children's books in the United States and Britain. The salespersons I spoke to in Lahore did not seem to know that these books were published in Delhi, although this omission may have been deliberate based on the assumption that people are less likely to buy Indian goods. Instead, they would often say that such books came from China or that they did not know the source of the books but keep them available because they are popular.

As in the case with headscarves, transnational connections were crucial in popularizing Good Word children's books in Lahore. They became known to people in Lahore through their relatives and friends settled abroad. One of my informants, a housewife and mother of two called Farida, had bought *Quran Stories for Little Hearts* books for her children after she saw her brother reading them to his children. He was settled in the United States and had asked her to send him some of the books as they are cheaper in Lahore. After mailing them via another relative who was traveling to the United States, she decided to buy them for her own children.

> I looked through the books and thought they were very good. They make you realize that Islam does not have to be taught in the same old boring way. It can be made *fun* and interesting. In the West, they are so good at teaching without making it tedious. Very different from our boring rote learning techniques.[38]

Another family—a couple with three children—whom I had met at an Islamic shop gave me a similar account of how they came across the books. They told me that the husband's sister lived in Canada and that she informed them of the books. Both of them liked the way the stories imparted important Islamic lessons to children, but in a new and interesting way. As the husband remarked to me,

> The Lessons stick in my children's mind. The books know how to reach out to children; they seem like ordinary stories, complete with pictures. They are easy to read and the lesson remains with you long after the story is finished. . . . Now we are all educated, our children can read and they should read and know about religion themselves. No one needs to tell them. These books make religion interesting and, at the same time, help you understand the essence of the message of Allah.

In the world occupied by new middle-class groups, parochial spells lack of progress and a sense of "being behind." In contrast, connections with, and awareness of, the outside world and global fashion trends symbolize individual agency, rational and forward thinking; in other words, a central definition of modernity. Within Pakistan, this idea of modernity has been propagated by the established elite and remains a way to preserve their dominant position. The playing field of modernity, in this context, is designed to favor the established. Even if upwardly mobile Lahoris learn English and are able to send their children to good schools or buy expensive Western goods, they remain a step behind the elite. Fostering links with a global Muslim community—a world outside Pakistan—allows the middle class to bypass this top layer of society and assert their modernity.

The desire in these emerging groups to associate themselves with a Muslim community beyond Pakistan corresponds to the deracination of Muslims in the West. The construction of an abstract global Muslim identity is largely a response to the contested place of Muslims in Western societies. For instance, as I discussed earlier in the book, Muslim communities in the United States often establish themselves as American by distancing themselves from the Islam of their homeland, and by aspiring to a homogenized and universal Islam.[39] Such a representation of Islam allows American Muslims to imagine themselves as part of a larger global community while, at the same time, allowing them to be thoroughly

American in their outlook. As Shryock astutely notes, universal Islam often "enshrines values that are consistent with enlightened middle-class American attitudes."[40] In a similar sense, as the patterns in religious consumption have illustrated, showing familiarity with the text is a way that aspiring groups try to break away from a parochial identity and toward a global one. In both cases, the use of modern education in building this global identity is particularly striking; for new middle-class Lahoris and diaspora Muslims alike, it is their literacy that allows them to build a relationship with the text and, through this, with an abstract global community.

Some general remarks on historical entanglements between particular and universalizing linkages of the Islamic world are relevant here. Engseng Ho's study of fourteenth-century Hadrami saiyid traders provides us with an example of the use of Islam by a particular group of people who became "active creators of a universal world."[41] Traveling across the Indian Ocean, the Hadrami saiyids created an expansive network of kin and relations by marrying women in different port towns. This allowed them to be accepted as family members in the different places they visited: Gujarat, Malabar, Malaysia, and Java. The Hadrami saiyids were able to hold these particular worlds together by their genealogical ties, linking them to each other, to the Prophet, and to a universal history of Islam. Through these chains, they were able to move between the particular and the universal. Genealogies, in this case, became a means of representation, to oneself and to others.[42] They connected the traders—who spent the majority of their lives at sea or abroad—to each other and to their home. At the same time, this genealogy linked them directly to the Prophet and, thus, allowed the saiyid traders to see themselves as the traveling light of the Prophet.[43] The Hadrami saiyids are just one example of this. Throughout the Muslim world, the saiyids were able to link a particular world to a universal one through their elevated genealogy. In South Asia for instance, many saiyids were Sufis who acted as intermediaries between lay people and Allah, and also as links to the larger world of Islam and Islamic knowledge.

In the twentieth century, this strategy of linking the particular with the universal ceased to be viable. The Hadrami saiyids lived in a world that privileged elevated genealogies and was held together by sacred languages.[44] With the rise of nationalism, elevated genealogies became a relic of the dynastic age and no longer enjoyed the same status. In a world where nation-states have become an almost natural category, genealogies cannot provide the same transnational linkages. Moreover, the world today is no longer held together by sacred languages; rather, national languages have emerged out of the strengthening of vernaculars. However, the Islamic case is interesting because it is still tied together by a common book and, associated with it, a sacred language. Genealogies may no longer be used to differentiate oneself from another or link oneself to a larger world, but another universal can be: education. Education has become a strategy for elevating oneself above others and also a way of connecting to the larger world of Islam. Whereas genealogy provided a way to create a link to the Prophet of Allah, education allows for a direct link to the text of Allah. In the contemporary world, it is the text that has become the Light. It links an individual to Allah, and individuals to each other.

The construction of this global Muslim identity—enabled by a familiarity with the text—has been influenced by the presence of an imagined outsider. Depending on the place and context, the outsider takes different forms: old-money groups in Pakistan, mainstream American society, or an abstracted West. One can even argue that in Lahore, the notion of a global Muslim has emerged in opposition to the established affluent and the imagined West; both groups, in the context of the postcolonial world, constituting the classic symbols of modernity. Although this position contests upper-class claims to modernity, it does not, however, challenge the prevailing conception of modernity itself. In fact, it appeals to largely the same ideals: connections to the outside world, economic prosperity and progress, buying power, and all of it facilitated by the favorite tool of the modernizing state: education and literacy. In other words, new middle-class groups in Lahore, as well diaspora Muslims in the West, are denigrated or marginalized for their lack of modernist values but, in turn, they use the very same methods and ideals to assert themselves. Moreover, the mode in which this identity and form of opposition is expressed has only been made possible by Western influence itself. In the final section, I turn to consumption in the month of *Ramazān* to show how the growing presence of multinational companies and increasing consumerism has allowed new middle-class families to consume goods and services—to "construct a lifestyle"—that were previously limited to established groups.

CONSUMING *RAMAZĀN* IN LAHORE

If middle-class consumers in Lahore use consumption to demonstrate their foreign connections, then the burgeoning advertisements of Pakistan also provide an "international feel" to its marketing campaigns. Advertisements on television and billboards in the city sell products by propagating the image of global Muslims, all believing in the same principles of Islam and all consuming the same goods. Other advertisements emphasize the transnational connections and links of the consumers. For instance, a popular television commercial by a local mobile phone operator shows a Pakistani couple in the United States. The woman holds a baby as the man picks up his mobile phone. The caller is the man's father, calling to whisper the *azān* in his grandson's ear.[45] The advertisement ends with a voiceover reminding viewers that no matter how far they are from their loved ones, traditions can be kept alive. While religion and the market economy combine on a daily basis to construct a modern Muslim lifestyle, at no time in the year is this more visible than during the month of *Ramazān*. During this period, local and multinational consumer brands, banks, restaurants, and the pious all come together to create a month of celebration, feasting, and, of course, fasting.

During the *Ramazān* of 2009, when I was in Lahore for fieldwork, the most popular special commercial of the year was produced by a local packaged milk company called Olpers. There was no escaping this advertisement: its background music was repeatedly played on the radio and in shops and restaurants. People frequently talked about the commercial and would flip channels on their televisions in the hope of catching it. The advertisement started with a voiceover that pronounces (in Urdu), "My fellow Muslims! In this blessed month, let's spread a message of peace. This is our quality, we are the selected people." On the screen, clips of different Muslim countries appear: a craftsman in Brunei, an artist in Pakistan, an engineer in Morocco, a dervish in Turkey, a doctor in Dubai, and a scientist in Egypt. These clips are followed by scenes from each of the selected countries, including people helping each other in daily life, praying together in congregations, and breaking their fasts at the same time. Glossy images of women and girls in headscarves are followed by clips of men and boys walking home from the mosque. In one snippet, a young man saves an older man from a pile of falling boxes. In another clip, he helps an old woman in a headscarf walk down a flight of stairs. These scenes are followed by images of people from different countries working diligently, before going home to pray and break the fast with their family. The pictures on the screen show the differences in Muslim appearances across the world, but concentrate on the unity of their faith and the similarity of their actions. At the end of the advertisement, the voiceover wishes all the viewers a prosperous, peaceful, and happy Eid. The background music for the commercial, sung by a local pop star, was a rendition of the song *Hum Mustafavī haiṅ* ("We Are the Selected Ones"), originally written and composed for the Second Summit of the Organization of the Islamic Countries in 1974. The chorus of the song gives the same message as the visual clips: *hum Mustafavī Mustafavī Mustafavī haiṅ*.[46]

There were many reasons why this commercial was popular. The background tune was particularly catchy. The pop star who sang it also appeared in the commercial. Since he is a local celebrity, many people watched the commercial multiple times just to see him. Some people also found the visual display appealing: the color and light synchronization was interestingly crafted, including a clip of one country blending very smoothly into a clip of a different country. For most, however, the commercial stood out because of the way it displayed Muslims. They liked the idea that the advertisement concentrated on the message of peace and brotherhood inherent in Islam. Although the advertisement was clearly made for a domestic audience, people appreciated the message that it was transmitting to the rest of the world, even if it was never established that anyone outside Pakistan—other than, perhaps, the Pakistani diaspora abroad—saw it. The global theme of the advertisement also appealed to the audience; it depicted all Muslims, despite the distances and the differences in their appearance, as part of the same community. Moreover, the beliefs and practices depicted were those that were largely compatible with the "modern" ethos of Islam, as propagated in pious circles.

This is what being Muslim means . . . we pray, we fast . . . but not just that. It is also about our belief and how we show that in our daily life . . . that we help others, we respect our elders. This is what our belief teaches us. And it is our belief that, despite our differences, brings us together.[47]

While the Olpers advertisement was an apt illustration of the world-view of middle-class Lahoris and their aspirations, for someone in Pakistan for the month of fasting after some years away, what was most striking was the opening message when the announcer wished the viewers a peaceful *Ramaẓān*.[48] Elsewhere, in many other advertisements and television programs, the sending and receiving of wishes for a happy and prosperous *Ramaẓān* was considered paramount. In 2009, sending *Ramaẓān* greeting text messages had become so commonplace that, on the eve of the first day of fasting, mobile phone networks were jammed by the heavy traffic. *Ramaẓān* has always been an auspicious month in Pakistan, yet most of the celebration (and consumption) surrounding it, until recently at least, centered around *īdu'l-fiṭr*, the day that marks the end of fasting. In recent years, however, the month of fasting itself has become an event—one that, more than ever before, is celebrated through consumption. Sending text messages the moment the moon is sighted, making use of special cheap call rates for the month, availing oneself of *ifṭār* and *saḥarī* deals at restaurants, and watching the special television shows are now some of the common ways of celebrating. As Figure 4.1 conveys, *Ramaẓān* is an event to be followed, watched, and consumed.

Other advertisements on billboards across the city are equally indicative of the culture of mass consumption that surrounds *Ramaẓān*. For instance, an advertisement by global fast-food chain KFC, extremely popular in Pakistan, announced special prices for the month by calling it *"Jashn-e-Ramadan,"* the festival or feast of *Ramaẓān* (Figure 4.2). A billboard of another popular international fast-food chain, whose logo is often called the "golden arches of American capitalism," advertised its *Ramaẓān* offers and a chance to win an *'umra* ticket by framing its campaign with the slogan "Priceless Blessings" (it was unclear whether the slogan was referring to the month or its special scheme; Figure 4.3). As in the construction of the holiday season surrounding Christmas,

Figure 4.1 A billboard advertising special *Ramaẓān* offers by an international mobile company. Photograph by the author.

multinational and local consumer goods companies have played an important role in constructing the festival of *Ramaẓān* in Pakistan.[49]

The "Christmasization" of Ramadan in Egypt has been well documented by Walter Armbrust and his analysis makes for a useful comparison here.[50] Armbrust is particularly relevant because his work examines Ramadan in relation to the rising presence of Islamism and in the context of a postcolonial society that, similar to Pakistan, sees connections to the outside as a defining aspect of modernity. In an article on the hegemony of Ramadan, Armbrust starts by explaining that although Egyptians do not necessarily make this distinction, what is considered as Ramadan in Egypt is actually now two Ramadans: one of fasting, prayer, and reflection and one of excessive consumption.[51] Ramadan in Egypt, he argues, is an instance of hegemony because it allows these two incompatible, and often contradictory forms, of the month to appear as naturalized. The hegemonic nature of Ramadan allows it to hold together changing social realties and interests. As Armbrust writes, "The reality

Figure 4.2 A billboard advertising special restaurant deals for the "festival" of *Ramaẓān*. Photograph by the author.

in question centers on the competition over meanings: the meaning of Egypt's relations to the world outside it, and the meaning of morality. These are sutured together by means of a ritual fused to a holiday, namely Ramadan."[52] While everyone in Cairo talks about Ramadan as a time of prayer and fasting—especially when confronted by an outsider—in practice, it is the Ramadan as a celebration that dominates. Armbrust reflects that

> the most obvious reason for this is that celebratory Ramadan practices in Egypt have long been co-opted by state modernizers and commercial interests, largely as a means of furthering what looks like an agenda of Westernization and secular materialism. But the point of an outwardly Westernized, secular or materialistic Ramadan is not to impose Westernization on Egyptian society. It is rather to buttress the position of

Figure 4.3 The priceless blessings of McDonald's. Photograph by the author.

those who control access to the outside by forming a hegemonic link to
the moral values inherent in the "universal Islam" [Ramadan as prayer
and fasting].[53]

Here, Armbrust turns to a discussion of a television program, one
which was immensely popular in 1980s among the aspiring middle-class
of Cairo. Titled *Fawazir Ramadan (Ramadan Riddles)*, the show aired
immediately following *iftār* and consisted of a series of riddles told
through "lavish highly publicized song-and-dance routines hosted by an
actress."[54] The correct answers to the riddles, sent to the Radio and
Television Union, were put into a lottery, with the winners receiving valu-
able prizes. As Armbrust argues, the television program brought together
several interests. It provided viewers with entertainment without any
apparent ideological content, while allowing the state to become the
master of the ceremony for the daily transition from sacred to profane
time and, in turn, to synchronize sacred time with commercial interest. In

effect, the program "fused a religious ritual with a free market-oriented ethic."[55] At the time, there were only three channels, making it possible for the government to control and arbitrate Ramadan television. Contrasting the 1980s with the last decade, Armbrust notes that with the rise of satellite television, there are now a multitude of channels with various Ramadan programs and, subsequently, the state is no longer the master of ceremony of the transition from sacred to profane times. The intertwining of commercial interest with religious celebration, however, continues and, if anything, is now far more pervasive.

Since the 1980s, visible signs of religiosity have also become common, especially in the middle-class areas in Cairo. Armbrust argues that such displays signify a shift away from the "state's vision of modern society—a society in which public signs of piety are rarely in evidence—towards a more Islamically oriented vision of society."[56] Given their inclination toward religion, and their nominal opposition to the state's vision, one would expect such groups to try to counter the hegemonic construct of Ramadan in Egypt. However, Armbrust finds that the Islamist position offers little alternative. The religiously inclined middle class may criticize the vulgarity of contemporary Ramadan television but they continue to watch it. Armbrust notes here that the "holiday fatigue" expressed by his informants was a sign of overconsumption rather than resistance. Meanwhile, the commercial interests of the state-backed elite and efforts to liberalize Egypt's economy are countered by shopping at department stores owned by Islamists rather than the secular elite. Most miss the irony that Islamist department stores have been able to flourish and expand because of the very same liberalized economy that Islamists otherwise criticize. Armbrust argues that the "fusing of a 'modern' form of Ramadan"—modern represented in this context by material prosperity—"with a timeless and 'true' form of Ramadan makes defining counter-hegemony extremely difficult."[57] As he explains, to be modern in Egypt requires an access to the outside:

> Modernity in Egypt is communicated through diacritica—public acts that communicate where a person stands in society; manners, clothes, ways of speaking; also habits of consumption, place of residence and the ability to move beyond Egypt and into the world outside. But this is a list

of publicly accessible resources rather than an index of progressively greater exclusion. One can buy the clothes at some level, and learn the manners and way of speaking. But not everyone can have the Mercedes, the villa, a position in a global business that pays world-class salaries, or the ability to be the broker of goods and services moving in and out of the country ... it is that power substantially equates to having access to wealthier economies, and access is strictly controlled.[58]

Middle-class Cairenes may have become more religious and display signs of conservatism but, at the same time, they are still "aspirants for a materially successful life (hence linked to having access to the outside world)."[59] Thus, they cannot completely resist the celebratory side of Ramadan.

Although Armbrust was discussing the difficulties of articulating a counter-hegemonic position to Ramadan in Cairo, he could have been discussing the problems inherent in the idea of modernity in Lahore and the challenges of establishing an alternative vision of it. As in Egypt, what is called *Ramaẓān* in Pakistan is actually two *Ramaẓān,* one of fasting and prayer, and the other of feasting and celebration. It is fair to say, however, that consumption in the month is not limited to the celebratory side alone. As noted earlier in this chapter, and to underscore a major point in my argument, self-representation in new middle-class groups ties together "true" religious belief with the "right" kind of religious consumption. Such linkages between religion and consumption are even more noticeable during *Ramaẓān* when there is an exponential rise in the sale of CDs and DVDs of television-based religious scholars as well as in the number of religious talk shows and television call-in shows. The predominant audience of the celebratory side of *Ramaẓān*—*ifṭār* deals, lottery prizes for *'umra* tickets, and special television dramas—is also the same middle class. Although most members of the upper class criticize "*Ramaẓān* hype" for becoming more garish by the year, that does not mean they do not participate. However, my argument is that the new middle class is the target audience for the types of advertisements discussed because they are more likely to consume such items in this month of the year. Unlike the affluent upper echelons of society who can—and certainly do—consume such products year-round, aspiring members of the new middle class wait for *Ramaẓān* for such consumption. Like the Cairenes that Armbrust describes, such middle-class Lahoris eat more in this month than at any other time of the year, and indulge themselves with restaurant visits and shopping.

Ramaẓān celebration and consumption has become an important feature of the emerging middle-class culture and one that is used to assert its presence in the social life of Lahore. Although the middle class sees itself in opposition to an abstracted West and the ideas and ideologies associated with it, the construction of this *Ramaẓān* culture has only been possible through the growth of the global market. In a society where connections to the outside establish one's position in the hierarchy of modernity, multinational and local corporate firms play a significant role in bringing this outside to the inside. Traditionally, the world outside has only been available to those at the top of Lahore's society and they have strictly controlled access to it. Whereas neoliberalism, as the growing presence of the market is often called, can be depicted as marginalizing, in this case it allows middle-class Lahoris to claim themselves as modern. Yet, in doing so, they buttress the elite definition of modernity that centers around a world outside Pakistan.

Conclusion

THROUGHOUT THIS BOOK, I have debated how relations between the established and new middle classes are mediated through, and draw upon, the history of modernization in Pakistan. As much as the established middle class is a product of the modernization program of the 1950s and 1960s—fragmented and short-lived as it was—it is the rendering of discourses and images associated with this time that shapes its identity in the present. In Lahore, nostalgia for this modernist past, and linkages with the history of progressivism in the subcontinent more broadly, convey both a social and a moral position. It allows individuals and families to establish themselves as part of the old middle class: an exhibition of tastes and sensibilities associated with modernism becomes a form of distinction, a way to separate oneself from new urban groups. But at the same time, such actions assert a moral claim of what modern life looks like and, indeed, what it means to be modern. Class hierarchies in Lahore, and in urban Pakistan more broadly, are value-laden with this moral claim of modernity. It is this claim that lies at the heart of middle-class politics and contests for status and social recognition in Lahore.

I have unraveled how, for new middle-class groups, socioeconomic mobility is viewed as a "move forward" within this larger moral universe. Class relations and hierarchies thus become a frame through which individuals gauge their own personal advancement over time, as well as a way to navigate their position vis-à-vis other groups. In this book, one of my central claims concerns how these struggles and aspirations are reflected in the new forms of piety noticeable among the emerging middle-class and upwardly mobile groups. Through a focus on the discussions in and around Quran schools and the reasons that people offer for following or distancing themselves from particular religious movements and scholars, I have argued that conceptions of an idealized pious self are not separate from broader aspirations for progress. Deliberations on what it means to be a "good Muslim" reveal an array of complex motivations, including both the desire for spiritual progress and an aspiration for becoming— and appearing to be—modern in relation to the wider moral universe. As much as ideas on idealized pious behavior are discovered through Islamic texts and learning, they are experienced and understood through one's position within the broader socioeconomic and moral hierarchies of Lahore. In this respect, I have also shown how these conceptions are by no means fixed, but change over time, through life experiences and in relation to other demands and expectations.

By drawing attention to this subjective flexibility, I have sought to reconsider the common sites of analysis for the study of contemporary religious life in Pakistan. In reaction to the alarm around the resurgence of religious identities in the Muslim world, as well as following a longer disciplinary history of academic work on South Asia, most recent scholarship has concentrated on a particular religious group or movement.[1] At the same time, there remains a tendency to conflate the conceptual aspects of these movements or sectarian affiliations with the lived experience of its followers. For instance, it is often assumed that identification or affiliation with a particular sect, such as Deobandi, Ahl-e-Sunnat, or Ahl-e-Hadis, represents a fixed set of views and positions. By contrast, the ethnography I have presented here on middle-class Lahore emphasizes the ambiguities across such sectarian and denominational boundaries of lived religious life. Despite identifying with either a particular religious group or none, I have described how most people's practices were formed through a variety of divergent sources. In most cases, the adoption of these different practices came without any changes in their larger religious affiliations. This was particularly noticeable in the views of women attending Quran schools, such as Al-Huda, who are often viewed as Wahhabi, but continue to identify themselves as belonging to the same *fiqh* as their families. In emphasizing these ambiguities, my intention is not to suggest that such sectarian identities have no contemporary relevance. Rather, it is to caution us from taking them as fixed and unchanging categories, as is often the case, in the analysis of religious life in Pakistan.

While current debates within the anthropology of Islam are largely concentrated on questions of fragmentation, this ethnography serves as a reminder that individual projects of ethical self-cultivation can sometimes bring together a diverse set of aspirations and goals. In their critique of the excessive focus on piety in recent literature, anthropologists have pointed out that religious aspirations often clash with other desires and obligations, leading to incoherence and fragmentation in everyday religious life.[2] The emphasis on a singular grand scheme for the organization of religious life and subjectification has thus been viewed as ignoring these contradictions. I have been attentive to these critiques via unravelling the ways in which aspirations to lead a pious life are entangled with struggles for upward mobility among new middle-class groups. In other words, a desire to be modern should be understood in relation to local hierarchies, but also in respect to the gaze of the world outside that views such groups as "backward."

However, departing from these works, I have also shown that these diverse aspirations and desires for self-making often do not lead to fragmentation and tensions, but are subsumed within a larger project of becoming a better Muslim. This is not to say that there are no spaces of ambivalence and tension; for instance, as discussed in Chapter 3, for many women attending Quran schools, religious aspirations often clash with familial obligations. Rather, paralleling Deeb, I have argued that pious ideals are discursively constructed in relation to, and in dialogue with, competing discourses and struggles.[3] Such intermingling points toward what Naveeda Khan has termed the "open" quality of Islam in Pakistan, but it is also the result of a long engagement of Islamic groups with broader political, social, and moral discourses. As elucidated in Chapter 2, social rhetoric in middle-class Lahore deploys the notion of *asl* Islam in a way that it is difficult to draw a distinction between what is moral, what is political, and what is religious. In this respect, more broadly, my ethnography underscores how the distinction between the "pious" and "everyday," implicitly made in the anthropology of Islam, is not always clear in lived experience.[4] This complexity may also hold for other parts of the Muslim world, and be one that anthropologists and social scientists more generally need to be cautious about when researching these sites.

Both the established and new middle-class groups are rooted in the sociohistorical specificity of urban Pakistan, and within a particular rendering of global modernization agendas. There is, however, a sense that both parties are "traveling through the West," to use Amitav Ghosh's phrase.[5] Throughout this book, the West appears in various garbs and forms: as a point of reference and appeal, a source of new ideas and lifestyles, and, most importantly, a frame through which to view oneself and others. Among new middle-class Lahoris, the West, appearing as an abstracted physical and ideological space, was a site for understanding and contesting their own marginality within local registers of status and modernity. The perception of Muslims as terrorists and irrational fanatics in the West, and the consequent discrimination against them, was often a focal point of new middle-class conversations. More often than not, such discourse was a vehicle for articulating distress about their own mistreatment at home by those in power, be it the state or more established urban groups. In such instances, the categories of the external outsider—the West—and the internal other overlap to produce an imagined audience that creates a sense of cultural intimacy for those being watched and condemned for their "backwardness." This idea of an outside audience is central to new middle-class self-representation, influencing not only religious attitudes but also the ways in which they are displayed through consumption. As much as these displays of self are pointed toward an abstract Western audience, they are also influenced by practices originating from the West. Here, the West and, in particular, Muslims abroad become a source of new ideas and connections. Through observing and holding discussions with family members in the West and with return-migrants—many of whom hold *dars* gatherings in their home—new middle-class Lahoris try to adopt practices that they perceive to bring them closer to *asl* Islam. In the process, they draw linkages with a global Muslim community, an overarching modern identity which allows them to move beyond and outside the social hierarchies of Lahore.

If, for aspiring groups, the West is a site of both opposition and opportunity in endeavors of self-making, it remains a reference point and source of legitimacy for the established middle class. Connections to the outside world, represented by proficiency in English, a taste for Western aesthetics and culture, and frequent travel abroad, bestow local status on the old middle class. Moreover, the old middle class derives its position as being viewed from the eyes of a Western audience. It is from the perspective of an outside world—a global stage which recognizes only the language of development—that the progressiveness of the established groups becomes imbued with a moral purpose that distinguishes them from other classes. Typically, the established middle class has been viewed as a harbinger of modernity in an otherwise beleaguered nation. In the post-9/11 context, however, the associated progressiveness has been inflected with the related purpose of warding off religious extremism and terrorism. This is a role that has been cast on to the established middle class by the world outside, but it is one that negotiates its relations with groups on the inside, such as the new middle class. In this sense, both the old and new middle-class groups are reminiscent of Amitav Ghosh's *In an Antique Land,* where he and his Egyptian hosts have much in common but are resigned to speak to one another through the language and values of the West. Much of the history that the old middle class nostalgically associates with itself—of a nation-state with some hope of modernity but dragged off course by an Islamizing military dictator—is the explanation given to an outside world for the rise of religious extremism in Pakistan. There is, of course, a historical truth here, but when attached to the normative claim of modernity, it becomes a narrative that has no space for the new middle class and its conception of a modern life.

Similar entanglements between the West, mass-mediated cultural intimacy, and self-representation are part of the reason why this new middle class is rarely explored in the academic study of Pakistan. While earlier literature on Pakistan largely centered on questions of growth, progress, and modernization, more recent areas of attention have predictably included the issues of security, terrorism, religious violence, and political instability. This literature addresses national and international policy concerns, while simultaneously shaping the way Pakistan is constructed in the mainstream Western imagination. In private conversations, public dialogues, or in academic settings, I am regularly faced with questions such as "what will happen to Pakistan?" or "how is Pakistan still surviving?". I am not alone in this situation: most Pakistan-focused academics who are based in Western centers of academia will identify with this experience and will have similar tales of how their own work and perspective are overshadowed by such questions and attitudes. Faced with this kind of audience, many academics fall back on explaining Pakistan through a narrative that identifies with the position of the established middle class.

Although security-related themes remain dominant, there has been a spate of recent academic work that departs from such concerns. Some of this literature has returned to "traditional" areas of academic inquiry in Muslim South Asia, such as intellectual histories of Islamic movements, Sufism, as well as the art and architecture of the regions. Other new works have focused on underexplored areas in the context of Pakistan studies, Partition politics, and on postindependence communist struggles and literary activism. The pervasiveness of this meta-narrative on Pakistan for the international audience is such that, although its intention may not be thus, the work is automatically categorized as the "other Pakistan." In this respect, it begins to support the nostalgic position of the established middle class and of what they and their Pakistan once was. Such accounts and positioning leave no room for a discussion of the contemporary aspiring and upwardly mobile groups, neither are they open to their social orientation and political attitudes. To redress this absence requires the academic community to reflect upon its own politics, and the connections and histories that it relies upon and holds dear, when writing about Pakistan on the international stage.

Notes

INTRODUCTION

1. Hamid et al. 2010.

2. Moretti writes that the latter emerged in eleventh-century French to describe residents of medieval towns *(bourgs)* who were free and exempt from feudal jurisdiction, and by the seventeenth century was used for "someone who belonged neither to the clergy nor to the nobility, did not work with his hands, and possessed independent means" (2014, 8). The term then surfaced in other European languages—for instance, *borghese* in Italian and *Bürger* in German.

3. Ibid, 11.

4. Ibid.

5. This was not least because genealogies were flexible and could change over the course of generations, but also because the *ashraf* included those who received state patronage in the form of titles and estates, or worked as legal administrators (Pernau 2013). Scholars, doctors, and religious teachers including Sufis—many of whom received state largesse—were also considered as *ashraf.*

6. Pernau 2013; Minault 1986.

7. See, e.g., Macaulay 1835.

8. For more on the linkages between the British and landed Muslim families in Punjab, see Talbot 1996. The term "gazetted" implies senior-level government employees, in particular, those who had the authority to issue an official stamp.

9. For a description of the socioeconomic and spatial shift toward middle-class status in colonial Lahore, see Daechsel 2006.

10. For India, see Dwyer 2000; Mankekar 1999. In recent years, the early decades after independence in Pakistan have received significant attention, but have been focused on left-wing groups and not on broader social composition. I address this literature in Chapter 1.

11. See, e.g., Asdar Ali 2015, 2016; Toor 2011.

12. See, e.g., Mahmood 2005; Schielke 2009; Soares 2005.

13. The term "Wahhabi" originates from Saudi Arabia, and refers to the reform movement associated with the teachings of Muhammad ibn Abd al-Wahhab (1703–1792). Wahhabism differs from mainstream Islamic thought on the fundamental issue of belief. Most Muslims, throughout history, have held the opinion that professing faith in Allah and Muhammad as his Prophet makes one a Muslim. However, Wahhabis believe that in order to qualify as a Muslim, one must affirm "absolutely and devote worship purely and exclusively to Allah. Any act of statement that indicates devotion to a being other than Allah is to associate another creature with Allah's power and that is tantamount to idolatry" (Commins 2006, vii). In South Asia, as in other parts of the Muslim world, the term "Wahhabi" is often used derogatively to imply heresy (see, e.g., Ahmed 1966). In contemporary Pakistan, it is used as a generic term to imply rigidity and extremist thinking. Jalal notes that the tendency to dub any Islamic revivalist movement in South Asia goes back to the nineteenth century where the British, wary of any religious or social upheaval, would dub any Islamic leader or movement that they feared might cause sedition as Wahhabi (2008, 137). The followers of al-Wahhab prefer to use the broader term *salafi*, although other self-professed *salafis* do not always accept them. *Salafi* is derived from *salaf*, used to refer to the first three generations of Muslims who are regarded as the most pure and knowledgeable of Muslims. The differences between *salafis* and orthodox Islamic scholars are complex but, in brief terms, revolve around the question of *taqlid*. In Islamic jurisprudence, *taqlid* (lit. "to follow" or "to imitate") refers to the acceptance of the verdict of established scholars of jurisprudence *(fiqh)* without asking for a detailed explanation or evidence of this opinion. However, *salafis* claim the right for interpreting the Quran and Sunna independently from established scholars of *fiqh*, and see *taqlid* as a "blind following of tradition." See, e.g., Hourani 1962, chaps. 5, 6, and 9; Kurzman 1998; Rahman 1982, chap. 2.

14. Muir 2016, 130.

15. Osella and Osella 2008a, 249. See also Osella and Osella 2008b; Soares and Osella 2009; Osella and Osella 2009.

16. For instance, historical work on the reformist Deoband movement has highlighted how the movement was not inimical to all forms of Sufism and, moreover, some of it leaders were also practicing Sufis. See, e.g., Metcalf 1982.

17. Osella and Osella 2008b, 318.

18. See, e.g., Huq 2008; Marsden 2005, 2008; Soares 2005.

19. Roy 2004.

20. Osella and Osella 2008b, 318.

21. Ibid.

22. Compare Deeb 2006, 2009.

23. For instances, see Roy 1992; Kepel 1985, 2002.

24. Deeb 2009, 113.

25. For a discussion of these assumptions, see Agrama 2011.

26. See, e.g., Mahmood 2005; Hirschkind 2006, 2005.

27. Deeb 2009, S112.

28. For Islam as a discursive tradition, see Asad 1986.

29. For fragmentation, see Schielke 2009; Osella and Osella 2009, 205.

30. Mahnaz Hussain, July 23, 2009.

31. Moreau and Hirsh 2007.

32. Steinberg 2015.

ONE: REMEMBERING A MODERN PAKISTAN

1. See, e.g., Pamük 2005, 2008.

2. Calvino 1997, 26.

3. Ahmad Kamal, January 1, 2010.

4. See, e.g., Boym 2001; Huyssen 1995, 2008.

5. Özyürek 2006, 11.

6. Calvino 1997.

7. Ansari's (2011) analysis of letters to the editor of the national daily news-paper, *The Dawn*, between 1950 and 1953 is revealing. She shows that five years after Partition, the urban public was bitterly disappointed by the provision of services and amenities, and criticized government officers for being corrupt, disorganized, and unwilling to serve the people.

8. Talbot 1998, 153.

9. For an illuminating account of the outlook of the military in Pakistan's formative years, and the social origins of its officers, see R. Moore 1969, 1979. For a broader discussion of the Pakistan Army, see Cohen 1984.

10. Gilman 2003, 3.

11. Talbot 1998; Noman 1988.

12. Spaulding 2003.

13. For instance, the master plan for Islamabad was made by the same architect who, a year before, had devised the plan for Baghdad's expansion. See, e.g., Pyla 2008.

14. Malik 2004, 75.

15. Sten Nilsson, quoted in Mumtaz 1985, 234.

16. Nilsson 1973, 166.

17. Eickelman 1989; see also Dresch 2000, Soares 2005.

18. Dresch 2000.

19. Lieven 2012, 66.

20. Shahzad 2009, 118.

21. Mujib-ur-Rehman, February 9, 2010.

22. Haroon Ghafoor, April 3, 2010.

23. Noman 1988, 41.

24. Akhter 2015.

25. Asdar Ali 2016, 107.

26. Gilmartin 1998, 2010; Jalal 1994.

27. Nelson 2009; Asdar Ali 2016.

28. Dadi 2010, 2016.

29. Toor 2011; Asdar Ali 2015, 2011a, 2011b, 2005.

30. Alavi 2003, 1988.

31. Asdar Ali 2015.

32. Ibid.

33. In Pakistan, housing projects are often referred to as housing schemes or societies. Typically, housing societies or schemes are developed by government agencies, or private parties, by acquiring rural land and dividing them into plots, some of which are allocated at a subsidized price to public officials (when it is a government scheme) or to the public by lottery. Others are sold at market value. This money is used to construct roads and lay down infrastructure for water, gas and electricity for the area. Samanabad is an example of an early housing scheme, where the government built houses that could be bought with an installment payment plan.

34. Dadi 2016.

35. Historians and political scientists have often read the ready acceptance of Urdu in Punjab, a province that receives the largest share of state resources, as part of a broader willingness to give up a Punjabi identity to gain a Pakistani one. While there is no doubt that Punjab has benefited, at the expense of other provinces, from being part of Pakistan, it should not be overlooked that there is a longer association between Urdu and urban life. Daechsel's (2006) work on nineteenth-century colonial Punjab highlights that reading and writing in Urdu was a distinct marker of middle-class identity at the time.

36. Dadi 2016.

37. Consider, for instance, the debates between the liberals, communists, and religious groups described by Toor (2011).

38. Berlant and Warner 1998, 549.

39. See, e.g., Ortner 1995.
40. See Shryock 2004; Herzfeld 1997.
41. Shryock 2004, 10.
42. Paracha 2012.
43. Wilk 1995, 111.
44. Doucet 2015; Preston 2015.
45. Tavernese 2010.
46. See, e.g., Siddiqa 2007; N. Ali 2013.
47. Siddiqa 2007, 197.
48. Quoted in Siddiqa 2007, 194.
49. Muhammad Aslam Rana, October 10, 2009.
50. Shahzad n.d., 145.
51. Haroon Ghafoor, April 3, 2010.
52. Kamil Khan Mumtaz, December 5, 2009.

TWO: MORAL RHETORIC, MODERNITY, AND CLASS

1. Glover 2007.

2. Shah 2005, 225.

3. Daechsel 2006.

4. Ibid.

5. However, following the Land Alienation Act of 1901, there were laws governing which tribes were allowed to own agricultural land. The act was part of a larger effort to maintain the status quo. After the experience of the war of 1857, the British were wary of changes in the social structure of the regions they governed and wanted to prevent changes in patterns of landholding. Based on the census, lists were drawn to determine whether a particular tribe could own agricultural land. However, this process crystallized what were previously rather fluid tribal identities. See, e.g., I. Ali 1988; Gilmartin 1988; Maqsood 2008.

6. Butalia 1998; Talbot 2006; Zamindar 2007.

7. Population Census Organization, www.census.gov.pk. http://www.pbs.gov .pk/sites/default/files//tables/District%20at%20a%20glance%20Lahore.pdf

8. R. Ali 2002; *Express Tribune* 2010; Shirazi and Kazmi 2014 It is estimated that by 2020, Lahore's population may exceed 11 million. Some recent government reports have suggested that Lahore's population has increased to 20 million, although these claims have been rejected by urban planners and commentators. See, e.g., Chaudhry 2017.

9. Migration to, and remittances from, the Gulf are an integral part of Pakistan's economy, and an important source of income for millions of families. In certain instances, the local economy of entire villages and semi-urban settlements

depend on income from relatives working in the Gulf. See Rashid and Gardezi 1983; Gilani, Khan,and Iqbal 1981; Batzlen 2000; Watkins 2009.

10. Maira 2008, 20.

11. Qadeer 2015.

12. Daechsel 2006.

13. Murphy 1996.

14. Murphy 2000, 211.

15. Ibid.

16. Ibid., 203.

17. Ibid., 211.

18. Salamandra 2004, 14.

19. Nasira Waheed, February 20, 2010.

20. Hasan 2002.

21. Bourdieu 1984.

22. Shaista Rahman, July 12, 2009. The term *ujaṛe nāwāb* refers to landed families that have either lost or, more often, squandered their wealth.

23. Ejaz Haider, May 4, 2010.

24. Iqbal Zaki, December 12, 2009.

25. Shahid Hussain, February 13, 2010.

26. Messiri 1978.

27. Robinson 2004.

28. Starrett 1998.

29. See, e.g., Hobsbawm and Ranger 1983.

30. Shahid Manzoor.

31. Jamshed Ahmed, January 9, 2010.

32. Compare Rollier 2010.

33. Compare Marsden 2005.

34. I. Ahmad 2008; Hirschkind 2006; Osella and Osella 2008.

35. Iqtidar 2012.

36. Khan 2012.

37. Although I agree with Khan that the inauguration of Pakistan constructed a space for Muslim striving, the centrality of Islam in her reading runs the risk of reproducing nationalist historiography where Islam is considered the raison d'être for the Partition. This ignores the historical narratives that suggest otherwise. Such an account runs the danger of producing history backward, in that it takes what is salient in everyday Pakistani life today and, subsequently, recasts it with historical certitude. Recent work has highlighted that in the early decades after Partition there were contested imaginings of Pakistan's future. The current predominance of one of these voices cannot retrospectively be equated with absence of others in the past.

38. Toor (2011) writes that as early as 1937 economic development was on the Muslim League's agenda.

39. Sivan 1985.

40. This description of Lahore's growth suggests that established groups—both the elite and prominent families of the past and the old middle class—tend to live in the east or southeast areas, while western parts are dominated by newer groups. However, spatial divisions do not neatly overlap with class cleavages. While most middle-class families of 1960s Samanabad have moved to other parts of the city, many of them continue to interact and socialize with friends and family members who have remained in their older neighborhood or in other nearby areas. Similarly, many long-term inhabitants of Model Town and Gulberg continue to live in such areas alongside new groups that have taken the place of those older families who have left for areas in the east of the city. Meanwhile, the DHA, now one of the most expensive residential areas in Lahore, is home to a variety of social groups and classes. Before the DHA was formed, some of the land within it was part of the Lahore Cantonment Housing Cooperative (LCCHS), a cooperative for retired military officers. At the time, plots within the cooperative were not very expensive and, in the late 1980s to early 1990s, were often bought up by incoming migrants from other parts of the country, return-migrants, and local upwardly mobile families.

41. Osella and Osella 2006.

42. Rahat Cheema, April 29, 2010.

43. Bourdieu 1977; Liechty 2003; Brosius 2012; Ganguly-Scrase and Scrase 2009.

44. Chanda Chugtai, March 23, 2010.

45. Deeb and Harb 2013, 17.

46. Ibid.

47. Ahmed Qureshi, March 3, 2014.

48. Ewing 1990.

49. Taimur Jibran, March 23, 2009.

50. Ibid., April 4, 2009.

51. *Nafs* refers both to the self and to the part of the self that desires and has appetites and passions (often called ego).

52. Iqtidar 2012, 6.

53. Ibid.

THREE: PIETY AND NEW MIDDLE-CLASS LIFE

1. Amina Ahsan, October 5, 2009. Personal *jāhil* means "ignorant" and is often used as a slur for someone who is considered uneducated or those who lack social etiquette and politeness. In addition, the word has historical significance

since the time before the coming of Prophet Muhammad is referred to as *jāhilīyat*, the age of ignorance.

2. In Pakistan, *maulā'ī* is used as a generic term for men involved in religious teaching and scholarship and in providing guidance on religious matters. It is also used, often derogatorily, to describe a person who is seen as overtly religious and prone to preaching. Jokes and stereotypes about *maulā'īs*—in particular, about their ignorance and greed—are common in Pakistan. Naveeda Khan (2012) has argued that such jokes about established religious authority are indicative of the skepticism that is part of Muslim striving in Pakistan. This was certainly the case in the example noted here, where my informant brought up the ignorance in relation to a broader idea on Islamic learning and practice.

3. Amina Ahsan, September 5, 2009.

4. Nina Khan, September 27, 2009.

5. Fareeha Jamshed, November 24, 2009.

6. Abeer Taimur, February 1, 2009.

7. Sajida Wasti, February 1, 2009.

8. Nuzhat Saleem, August 9, 2009.

9. Nuzhat Saleem, September 12, 2009.

10. Leena Raza, January 4, 2010.

11. Seema Rahim, January 4, 2010.

12. Annie Alvi, January 4, 2010.

13. See, e.g., Still 2011; Jeffery, Jeffery, and Jeffery 2004.

14. See, e.g., Starrett 1998.

15. For a detailed ethnography of the Jamaat and its alliance with Zia's martial law, see Nasr 1993, 1994.

16. S. Ahmad 2009.

17. There is some controversy regarding Hashmi's claim that she earned her PhD from the University of Glasgow. Many of her critics in the Pakistani media have argued that she never completed the degree but have been unable to provide evidence. In a personal communication with the author, Dr. Usha Sanyal, a historian of South Asian religious movements, mentioned that in 2011 she tried to obtain a copy of Hashmi's thesis from the University of Glasgow but it was not listed in the central database. Since then, she has been in contact with Hashmi who agreed to send her a copy of the thesis but has not done so as yet.

18. S. Ali 2002.

19. Farah Azhar, September 27, 2009.

20. See, e.g., Schielke 2009.

21. In scholarship on Sunnī Islam, *fiqh* refers to the four schools of jurisprudence—Hanafi, Shafi, Maliki, and Hanbali—based on the works of Great Imams who systematized the science of Islamic jurisprudence between the eighth

and nineth centuries (see Hallaq 1997, 2009). In Pakistan, most people belong to Hanafi *fiqh*. However, when ordinary people speak of *fiqh*, they are usually referring to denominations within the Hanafi school (particularly Deobandi or Barelwi) or in terms of sects (for instance, Sunnī and Shi'as Islam are referred to as the two dominant *fiqh*). Rarely do discussions of *fiqh* extend to Maliki, Hanbali, and Shafi schools.

22. See, e.g., Ewing and Hoyler 2008; Maira 2008; Shryock 2008a, 2008b.

23. Shryock 2008a, 204.

24. Armbrust 2002a, 925.

25. Afifa Omar, December 19, 2013.

26. Rubina Farhan, November 15, 2009.

27. Compare Schielke 2009.

28. Saima Abbas, March 13, 2010.

29. Afshan Attique, March 13, 2010.

30. Sajida Wasti, March 13, 2010.

31. Compare Huq 2008.

32. Fatima Hamid, December 1, 2013.

33. Rehana Karamat, December 5, 2013.

34. Mahmood 2004, 88.

35. Mehreen Ali, April 4, 2010.

36. In colloquial Urdu, *khānā purī* (lit. "ticking boxes") describes moments or actions when something is done for the sake of formalities.

37. Amina Ahsan, March 7, 2010.

38. Rubina Farhan, November 15, 2009.

39. For a general discussion, see Agrama 2011; Asad 1993. For a South Asia–specific discussion, see Iqtidar 2012.

40. Limbert 2005, 184–185.

41. Starrett 1998.

42. Mahmood 2004, 90.

43. Ibid.

44. *Namehram* refers to men and women who one could potentially marry. For instance, under Islamic law, a woman cannot marry her father, brother, son, and uncles. Anyone falling outside this category is *namehram*.

45. Mariyam Zaman, August 1, 2010.

46. See, e.g., Messick 1993.

47. See, e.g., I. Ahmad 2011; Zaman 2002.

48. See, e.g., Sikand 2011.

49. Ayesha Nisar, August 28, 2009.

50. The six points which form the core of the Tablighi Jamaat's work are *īmān* (faith), *salāt* (daily prayers), *ilm-o-zikr* (knowledge and recitation/praise of Allah),

ikrām al Muslimīn (duty towards and sacrifice for other Muslims), *ikhlāṣ* (respect and love for others), and *dāwā* (preaching).

51. Ayesha Nisar, August 28, 2009.

52. Compare Soares 2005.

53. Samra Shaukat, December 17, 2009.

54. Devji 2007.

55. I have borrowed the term "overstanding" from literary theory, where it was introduced by Wayne Booth (1979) but later used and developed by William Mitchell (1987) and Raymond Tallis (1995, 2008). Mitchell explains overstanding involves "not just 'commentary' or 'interpretation' of primary texts, but to clarify fundamental questions about the nature of literature, its relations to other arts, its place in the whole fabric of cultural, social, and political reality" (Mitchell 1987, 16). I use the term to reflect upon a similar tendency in interpreting the Quran.

56. For parallels between Zakir Naik's speaking style and televangelism, see Larkin 2008.

57. Zakir Naik had to deliver this lecture via satellite rather than in person because he was denied a British visa; it is available on YouTube at http://www .youtube.com/watch?v=e594FaHPPrc.

FOUR: ISLAM AND CONSUMPTION

1. Starrett 1995, 53.

2. Jones 2007, 2010a, 2010b; Abaza 2007; Moors 2007; Tarlo 2010.

3. See, e.g., Starrett 1996; Yaqin 2007; Meneley 2007; Armbrust 2002b.

4. Sanyal 1999, 144.

5. See, e.g., Lewis 2010.

6. For Muslim houses, see McCloud 1996.

7. Jones 2007, 2010a, 2010b; Meneley 2007.

8. Fischer 2010.

9. Samina Rahman, September 29, 2009.

10. In Pakistan, as in other parts of the Muslim world, Islamic banking is meant to be interest free. In the case of debit cards, this is achieved by not offering overdraft services.

11. *Ḥamd* refers to poetry or song praising Allah whereas *na'ats* are songs celebrating the Prophet.

12. Yusuf Sami is a British-born Muslim singer, known for singing Islamic "rock songs" that have attracted a large Muslim following. Sami calls his genre of music "spiritique."

13. Ahmed Khan, October 23, 2009.

14. Kepel 1985; Roy 1992; Eickelman and Piscatori 1996.

15. The linkages between economic liberalization and Islamic consumption has been extensively covered in the case of Turkey. See, e.g., Özyürek 2004, 2006; Navaro-Yashin 2002a, 2002b; Sandikçi and Ger 2001, 2007.

16. There are approximately 100 private entertainment and news channels operating in Pakistan. According to government legislation, all private channels need to be licensed by the Pakistan Electronic Media Regulating Authority (PEMRA). In practice, however, many channels continue to operate illegally.

17. The Mecca-Cola available in Pakistan was locally produced, but it was an imitation of a drink of the same name produced by Mecca-Cola World Company, owned by a French Muslim, Tawfiq Mathlouthi. The original Mecca-Cola was produced in the early 2000s and is predominantly sold in Muslim neighborhoods in Paris as well as in British cities that have a large Muslim population, such as Birmingham. Although the company is originally French, it has its headquarters in Dubai. The popularity in Pakistan of Mecca-Cola, an imitation of a drink produced in France but consumed in Britain and based in Dubai, shows the international connections that are often involved in the construction of Muslim tastes, a theme that I will discuss in a later section in this chapter.

18. Yaqin 2007, 185.

19. Swartz 1997, 163.

20. Wacquant 2012, 68.

21. For more on fortune-telling parrots, see Pinault 2008.

22. Water from the well of Zam Zam, located inside the Masjid Al-Haram in Saudi Arabia, is called āb-e-zam zam. It is believed that the water appeared at this site when Abraham's young son Ishmael kicked the ground while crying from thirst. Depicted as a miracle of God, the water is considered to hold miraculous properties of healing and well-being.

23. Mohammad Karim, October 28, 2009.

24. Rashid Jatt, September 26, 2009.

25. Khosravi 2008

26. Hasan Mahmood, September 26, 2009.

27. Chanda Chugtai, October 1, 2009.

28. Qasim Butt, October 3, 3009.

29. Hyder (2006) has argued that religious instruction at home often exposes children to various Islamic discourses ranging from classical texts to poetry and songs. In comparison to this, diaspora Muslims who undergo formal religious instruction are only exposed to classical texts and often develop a more reified rigid understanding of Islam. For these diaspora Muslims, Muslims at home are often seen to be following a vague and ambiguous Islam, dangerously close to mere "custom."

30. Chanda Chugtai, October 1, 2009.

31. Tarlo 2010, 118.

32. Lit. means "to veil" or "veiled."

33. Chanda Chugtai, October 1, 2009. *Dupaṭṭā* is a long scarf that most Pakistan women wear over their shoulders or head.

34. *Paindū* is a Punjabi word, derogatorily used to refer to someone who is "backward," unfashionable. It is sometimes used by people in urban areas when referring to someone from a rural location.

35. Chanda Chugtai, October 20, 2009.

36. Ayesha Ansari, October 29, 2009.

37. Yaqoob Khalili, September 17, 2009.

38. Farida Amir, October 13, 2010.

39. See, e.g., Ewing and Hoyler 2008; Shryock 2008a, 2008b.

40. Shryock 2008a, 204.

41. Ho 2007, 348.

42. Ibid., 350.

43. The idea of the Prophet Muhammad as the Light is common across the Muslim world. In South Asia, the common practice among Barelwi and some Sufi denominations of kissing their hands and touching them to their foreheads whenever the Prophet's name is mentioned is a way of acknowledging this Light.

44. See Anderson 1983.

45. In Islam, the *azān* is whispered in a newborn's ears to symbolize that she/he is a Muslim and born in a Muslim household.

46. Derived from the root word *Mustafa* (one of the names given to the Prophet), *Mustafavī* literally means "lordly" or the "selected one." It is usually used to denote Muslims.

47. Farida Amir, October 13, 2010.

48. Earlier ethnographies have noted similar shifts between localism and universalism in festivities in the Muslim world; see Peters 1976; Fallers and Fallers 1974.

49. Compare Miller 1993.

50. Armbrust 2007, 2005, 2002b.

51. Armbrust 2007, 156.

52. Ibid., 158.

53. Ibid, 163

54. Ibid., 165.

55. Ibid.

56. Ibid., 167.

57. Ibid.

58. Ibid., 171.

59. Ibid.

CONCLUSION

1. I refer here to the large body of historical work focusing on nineteenth-century reform movements in Muslim South Asia, for instance, Metcalf 1992; Robinson 2001. This work has been seminal in our understanding of reform movements and religious scholars of the time but, simultaneously, its eminence has meant that later work has followed the same trend and focused on scholars and movements, rather than on the practices of ordinary followers and laypersons.

2. Schielke 2009.

3. Khan 2012.

4. See, for instance, the debate among Samuli Schielke, Lara Deeb, Nadia Fadil, and Mayanthi Fernando on the pious and the everyday in Deeb 2015; Fadil and Fernando 2015.

5. Ghosh 1992, 36.

Bibliography

Abaza, Mona. 2007. "Shifting Landscapes of Fashion in Contemporary Egypt."
    Fashion Theory: The Journal of *Dress, Body, and Culture* 11(2–3): 281–97. doi:
    10.2752/136270407X202817.

Agrama, Hussein Ali. 2011. *Questioning Secularism: Islam, Sovereignty, and the*
    Rule of Law in Modern Egypt. Chicago: University of Chicago Press.

Ahmad, Irfan. 2008. "Cracks in the 'Mightiest Fortress': Jamaat-e-Islami's
    Changing Discourse on Women." *Modern Asian Studies* 42: 549–75. doi:
    10.1017/S0026749X07003101.

———. 2011. "Immanent Critique and Islam: Anthropological Reflections."
    Anthropological Theory 11: 107–32. doi: 10.1177/1463499611398188.

Ahmad, Sadaf. 2009. *Transforming Faith: The Story of Al-Huda and Islamic Revival*
    among Urban Pakistani Women. Syracuse, NY: Syracuse University Press.

Ahmed, Qeyamuddin. 1966. *The Wahhabi Movement in India.* Calcutta: Firma
    K. L. Mukhopadhyay.

Akhter, Majed. 2015. "The Hydropolitical Cold War: The Indus Water Treaty
    and State Formation in Pakistan." *Political Geography* 46: 65–75. doi:
    10.1016/j.polgeo.2014.12.002.

Alavi, Hamza. 1988. "Pakistan and Islam: Ethnicity and Ideology." In *State and*
    Ideology in the Middle East and Pakistan, edited by Hamza Alavi and Fred
    Halliday. New York: Monthly Review Press.

———. 2003. "Social Forces and Ideology in the Making of Pakistan." In *Continuity and Change: Sociopolitical and Institutional Dynamics in Pakistan,* edited by Syed Akbar Zaidi. Karachi: City Press.

Ali, Imran. 1988. *The Punjab under Imperialism, 1885–1947.* Princeton, NJ: Princeton University Press.

Ali, Nosheen. 2013. "Grounding Militarism: Structures of Feeling and Force in Gilgit-Baltistan." In *Everyday Occupations: Experiencing Militarism in South Asia and the Middle East,* edited by Kamala Visweswaran. Philadelphia: University of Pennsylvania Press.

Ali, Reza. 2002. "Underestimating Urbanization." *Economic and Political Weekly.* 37(44–45): 4544–55.

Ali, Sahar. 2002. "Pakistani Women Socialites Embrace Islam." *BBC South Asia,* November 6. http://news.bbc.co.uk/2/hi/south_asia/3211131.stm.

Anderson, Benedict. 1983. *Imagined Communities: Reflections on the Origin and Spread of Nationalism.* London: Verso.

Ansari, Saira. 2011. "Everyday Expectations of the State during Pakistan's Early Years: Letters to the Editor, *Dawn* (Karachi), 1950–1953." *Modern Asian Studies* 45(1): 159–78. doi:10.1017/S0026749X10000296.

Armbrust, Walter. 2002a. "Islamists in Egyptian Cinema." *American Anthropologist* 104 (3): 922–31. http://www.jstor.org/stable/3567266.

———. 2002b. "The Riddle of Ramadan: Media, Consumer Culture, and the 'Christmasization' of a Muslim Holiday." In *Everyday Life in the Middle East* (rev. ed.), edited by Donna Bowen and Evelyn Early. Bloomington: Indiana University Press.

———. 2005. "Synchronizing Watches: The State, the Consumer, and Sacred Time in Ramadan Television." In Meyer and Moors, chap. 10.

———. 2007. "Celebratory Ramadan and Hyperpiety in a Mexican Standoff: Counterhegemony in the Crossfire." In *Counterhegemony in the Colony and Postcolony,* edited by John Chalcraft and Yaseen Noorani. London: Palgrave Macmillan.

Asad, Talal. 1986. *The Idea of an Anthropology of Islam* (occasional paper series). Washington, DC: Georgetown University Center for Contemporary Arab Studies.

———. 1993. *Genealogies of Religion: Discipline and Reasons of Power in Christianity and Islam.* Baltimore: John Hopkins University Press.

Asdar Ali, Kamran. 2005. "Strength of the State Meets the Strength of the Street: The 1972 Labor Struggle in Karachi." *International Journal of Middle East Studies* 37: 83–107. https://www.jstor.org/stable/3880083.

———. 2011a. "Progressives and 'Perverts': Partition Stories and Pakistan's Future." *Social Text* 29(3): 1–29. doi: 10.1215/01642472-1299947.

————. 2011b. "Communists in a Muslim Land: Cultural Debates in Pakistan's Early Years." *Modern Asian Studies* 45(3): 501–34. doi: 10.1017/S0026749X11000175.

————. 2015. *Communism in Pakistan: Politics and Class Activism 1947–1972.* London: Tauris.

————. 2016. "Cinema and the City." In Khan and Ahmad, chap. 4.

Berlant, Lauren, and Michael Warner. 1998. "Sex in Public." *Critical Inquiry* 24(2): 547–66.

Booth, Wayne. 1979. *Critical Understanding: The Powers and Limits of Pluralism.* Chicago: University of Chicago Press.

Bourdieu, Pierre. 1984. *Distinction: A Social Critique of the Judgment of Taste,* translated by R. Nice. Cambridge, MA: Harvard University Press.

Boym, Svetlana. 2001. *The Future of Nostalgia.* New York: Basic Books.

Brosius, Christiane. 2010. *India's Middle Class: New Forms of Urban Leisure, Consumption and Prosperity.* London: Routledge.

Butalia, Urvashi. 1998. *The Other Side of Silence: Voices from the Partition of India.* New Delhi: Penguin Books.

Calvino, Italo. 1997. *Invisible Cities.* London: Seeker and Warburg.

Chaudhry, Asif. 2017. "'Scheme' to divide Lahore into four dists in the works." *Dawn,* April 26. https://www.dawn.com/news/1329295.

Cohen, Stephen. 1984. *The Pakistan Army.* Berkeley: University of California Press.

Commins, David. 2006. *The Wahhabi Mission and Saudi Arabia.* London: Tauris.

Dadi, Iftikhar. 2010. "Registering Crisis: Ethnicity in Pakistani Cinema of the 1960s and 1970s." In Khan, chap. 5.

————. 2016. "Modernity and Vernacular Cinema." In Khan and Ahmad, chap. 3.

Daechsel, Markus. 2006. *The Politics of Self-Expression: The Urdu Middle Class Milieu in Mid-Twentieth Century India and Pakistan.* London: Routledge.

Deeb, Lara. 2006. *An Enchanted Modern: Gender and Public Piety in Shi'i Lebanon.* Princeton, NJ: Princeton University Press.

————. 2009. "Piety Politics and the Role of a Transnational Feminist Analysis." *The Journal of the Royal Anthropological Institute* 15 (Islam, Politics, Anthropology): 112–26. http://www.jstor.org/stable/20527692.

————, and Mona Harb. 2013. *Leisurely Islam: Negotiating Geography and Morality in Shi'ite South Beirut.* Princeton, NJ: Princeton University Press.

————. 2015. "Thinking Piety and the Everyday Together: A Response to Fadil and Fernando." *Hau* 5(2): 93–96. doi:10.14318/hau5.2.007.

Devji, Faisal. 2007. "Apologetic Modernity." *Modern Intellectual History* 4(1): 61–76. doi:10.1017/S1479244306001041.

Doucet, Lyse. 2015. "Lahore Literary Festival: Book Lovers Defy the Bombers."
    BBC.com, February 24. http://www.bbc.com/news/world-asia-31602457.
Dresch, Paul. 2000. *A History of Modern Yemen.* Cambridge: Cambridge
    University Press.
———, and James P. Piscatori, eds., *Monarchies and Nations: Globalization and
    Identity in the Arab States of the Gulf.* London: Tauris.
Dwyer, Rachel. 2000. *All You Want Is Money, All You Need Is Love: Sexuality and
    Romance in Modern India.* London: Cassell.
Eickelman, Dale. 1989. "National Identity and Religious Discourse in Contemporary
    Oman." *International Journal of Islamic and Arabic Studies* 6: 1–20.
———, and James Piscatori. 1996. *Muslim Politics.* Princeton, NJ: Princeton
    University Press.
Ewing, Katherine. 1990. "The Illusion of Wholeness: Culture, Self, and the
    Experience of Inconsistency." *Ethos* 18: 251–78. http://www.jstor.org/
    stable/640337.
———, ed. 2008. *Being and Belonging: Muslims in the United States since 9/11.*
    New York: Russell Sage Foundation.
———, and Marguerite Hoyler. 2008. "Being Muslim and American: South
    Asian Muslim Youth and the War on Terror." In Ewing, 80–104.
Express Tribune. 2010. "Lahore to Be Home to 11.25m Come 2020." *The Express
    Tribune,* July 11. http://tribune.com.pk/story/27025/ lahore-to-be-home-to
    -11–25m-come-2020/.
Fadil, Nadia, and Mayanthi Fernando. 2015. "Rediscovering the 'Everyday'
    Muslim: Notes on an Anthropological Divide." *Hau* 5(2): 59–88.
    doi:10.14318/hau5.2.005.
———. 2015. "What Is Anthropology's Object of Study? A Counterresponse to
    Deeb and Schielke." *Hau* 5(2): 97–100. doi:10.14318/hau5.2.008.
Fallers, Lloyds, and Margaret Fallers. 1974. "Notes on an Advent Ramadan."
    Journal of the American Academy of Religion 42(1): 35–52. http://www.jstor
    .org/stable/1461526.
Fischer, Johan. 2010. "Boycott or Buycott? Malay Middle-Class Consumption
    Post-9/11." *Ethnos* 75(1): 29–50. doi:10.1080/0014184070121950.
Ganguly-Scrase, Ruchira, and Scrase, Timothy J. 2008. *Globalization and the
    Middle Classes in India: The Impact of Neoliberal Reforms.* London: Routledge.
Gans, Herbert. 1982. *The Urban Villagers: Group and Class in the Life of Italian-
    Americans.* New York: Free Books.
Ghosh, Amitav. 1992. *In an Antique Land.* London: Granta Books.
Gilani, Ijaz, Fahim Khan, and Munawar Iqbal. 1981. *Labour Migration from
    Pakistan to the Middle East and Its Impact on the Domestic Economy.*
    Islamabad: Pakistan Institute of Development Economics.

Gilman, Nils. 2003. *Mandarins of the Future: Modernization Theory in Cold War America.* Baltimore: John Hopkins University Press.

Gilmartin, David. 1988. *Empire and Islam: Punjab and the Making of Pakistan.* London: Tauris.

———. 1998. "Partition, Pakistan, and South Asian History: In Search of a Narrative." *The Journal of Asian Studies* 57(4): 1068–95. http://www.jstor.org /stable/26959304.

———. 2010. "Living the Tensions of the State, the Nation, and Everyday Life." In Khan, afterword. London: Routledge.

Glover, William. 2007. *Making Lahore Modern: Constructing and Imagining a Colonial City.* Minneapolis: University of Minnesota Press.

Hallaq, Wael. 1997. *A History of Islamic Legal Theories: An Introduction to Sunnī uṣūl al-fiqh.* New York. Cambridge University Press.

———. 2009. *Sharī'a: Theory, Practice and Transformations.* Cambridge: Cambridge University Press.

Hamid, Mohsin, Mohammed Hanif, Daniyal Mueenuddin, and Kamila Shamsie. 2010. "How to Write about Pakistan." *Granta* 112: Pakistan Online, September 28. http://granta.com/how-to-write-about-pakistan/.

Hasan, Arif. 2002. "The Roots of Elite Alienation." *Economic and Political Weekly* 37 (44–45): 4550–4553.

Herzfeld, Michael. 1997. *Cultural Intimacy: Social Poetics in the Nation-State.* New York: Routledge.

Hirschkind, Charles. 2005. "Cassette Ethics: Public Piety and Popular Media in Egypt." In Meyer and Moors, chap. 1.

———. 2006. *The Ethical Soundscape: Cassette Sermons and Islamic Counterpublics.* New York: Columbia University Press.

Ho, Engseng. 2007. "The Two Arms of Cambay: Diasporic Texts of Ecumenical Islam in the Indian Ocean." *Journal of the Economic and Social History of the Orient* 50(2): 347–61. http://www.jstor.org/stable/25165199.

Hobsbawm, Eric J., and Terence Ranger, eds. 1983. *The Invention of Tradition.* Cambridge: Cambridge University Press.

Hourani, Albert. 1962. *Arabic Thought in the Liberal Age, 1798–1939.* Oxford: Oxford University Press.

Huq, Maimuna. 2008. "Reading the Qur'an in Bangladesh: The Politics of 'Belief' among Islamist Women." *Modern Asian Studies* 42: 457–88. doi:10.1017/S00 26749X07003149.

Huyssen, Andreas. 1995. *Twilight Memories: Marking Time in a Culture of Amnesia.* London: Routledge.

———. 2008. *Other Cities, Other Worlds: Urban Imaginaries in a Global World.* Durham, NC: Duke University Press.

Hyder, Syed Akbar. 2006. *Reliving Karbala: Martyrdom in South Asian Memory.*
    Oxford: New York.
Iqtidar, Humeira. 2012. *Secularizing Islamists? Jama'at-e-Islami and Jama'at-ud-
    Da'wa in Urban Pakistan.* Chicago: University of Chicago Press.
Jalal, Ayesha. 1994. *The Sole Spokesman: Jinnah, the Muslim League, and the
    Demand for Pakistan.* Cambridge: Cambridge University Press.
———. 2008. *The Partisans of Allah: Jihad in South Asia.* Lahore: Sang-e-Meel
    Publications.
Jeffery, Craig, Patricia Jeffrey, and Roger Jeffrey. 2004. "'A Useless Thing!' or
    'Nectar of the Gods?' The Cultural Production of Education and Young
    Men's Struggle for Respect in Liberalizing North India." *Annals of the
    Association of American Geographers* 94(4): 961–81. http://www.jstor.org
    /stable/3694106.
Jones, Carla. 2007. "Fashion and Faith in Urban Indonesia." *Fashion Theory: The
    Journal of Dress, Body, and Culture* 11(2–3): 211–31. doi:10.2752
    /136270407X202763.
———. 2010a. "Images of Desire: Creating Virtue and Value in an Indonesian
    Islamic Lifestyle Magazine." *Journal of Middle East Women's Studies* 6(3):
    91–117. doi:10.2979/mew.2010.6.3.91
———. 2010b. "Materializing Piety: Gendered Anxieties about Faithful
    Consumption in Contemporary Urban Indonesia." *American Ethnologist*
    37(4): 617–37. doi:10.1111/j.1548–1425.2010.01275.x.
Kepel, Gilles. 1985. *The Prophet and the Pharaoh: Islamic Extremism in Egypt.*
    London: Al-Saqi Books.
———. 2002. *Jihad: The Trail of Political Islam.* London: Tauris.
Khan, Ali, and Ali Nobil Ahmad, eds. 2016. *Cinema and Society: Film and Social
    Change in Pakistan.* Karachi: Oxford University Press.
Khan, Naveeda, ed. 2010. *Pakistan: Beyond Crisis.* London: Routledge.
———. 2012. *Muslim Becoming: Aspiration and Skepticism in Pakistan.* Durham,
    NC: Duke University Press.
Khosravi, Shahram. 2008. *Young and Defiant in Tehran.* Philadelphia: University
    of Pennsylvania Press.
Kurzman, Charles. 1998. *Liberal Islam: A Source Book.* Oxford: Oxford University
    Press.
Larkin, Brian. 2008. "Ahmed Deedat and the Form of Islamic Revivalism." *Social
    Text* 26(3): 101–21. doi:10.1215/01642472–2008–006.
Lewis, Reina. 2010. "Marketing Muslim Lifestyle: A New Media Genre." *Journal
    of Middle East Women's Studies* 6(3): 58–90. doi:10.2979/mew.2010.6.3.58.
Liechty, Mark. 2003. *Suitably Modern: Making Middle-Class Culture in a New
    Consumer Society.* Princeton, NJ: Princeton University Press.

Lieven, Anatol. 2012. *Pakistan: A Hard Country*. London: Penguin Books.

Limbert, Mandana E. 2005. "Gender and Religious Education in Oman." In Dresch and Piscatori, 182–202.

Macaulay, Thomas. 1835. *Minute on Indian Education*. www.msu.edu/projectsouthasia.

Mahmood, Saba. 2004. *Politics of Piety: The Islamic Revival and the Feminist Subject*. Princeton, NJ: Princeton University Press.

Maira, Sunaina. 2008. "Citizenship, Dissent, Empire: South Asian Muslim Immigrant Youth." In Ewing, 15–46.

Malik, Ayyub. 2004. "Postcolonial Capitals of South Asia: A Critical Analysis of Chandigarh, Dhaka and Islamabad" (conference and exhibition report). *Global Built Environment Review* 3(1): 68–80.

Mankekar, Purnima.1999. *Screening Culture, Viewing Politics: An Ethnography of Television, Womanhood, and Nation in Postcolonial India*. Durham, NC: Duke University Press.

Maqsood, Ammara. 2008. *The 'Ethnographic State' and Colonial Punjab: The Construction of 'Tribal' Identities*. Unpublished MPhil Thesis, University of Oxford.

Marsden, Magnus. 2005. *Living Islam: Muslim Religious Experience in Pakistan's North-West Frontier Province*. Cambridge: Cambridge University Press.

———. 2008. "Women, Politics, and Islamism in Northern Pakistan." *Modern Asian Studies* 42: 405–29. http://www.jstor.org/stable/20488025.

McLeod, Arlene. 1991. *Accommodating Protest: Working Women, the New Veiling, and Change in Cairo*. New York: Columbia University Press.

Meneley, Anne 2007. "Fashions and Fundamentalism in Fin-de-Siècle Yemen: Chador Barbie and Islamic Socks." *Cultural Anthropology* 22(2): 214–43. doi: 10.1525/can.2007.22.2.214.

Messick, Brinkley. 1993. *The Calligraphic State: Textual Domination and History in a Muslim Society*. Berkeley: University of California Press.

Messiri, Sawsan. 1978. *Ibn-balad: A Concept of Egyptian Identity*. Leiden: Brill.

Metcalf, Barbara. 1982. *Islamic Revival in British India: Deoband, 1860–1900*. Delhi: Oxford University Press.

Meyer, Birgit, and Annelies Moors, eds. 2005. *Religion, Media, and the Public Sphere*. Bloomington: Indiana University Press.

Miller, Daniel, ed. 1993. *Unwrapping Christmas*. Oxford: Clarendon Press.

Minault, Gail. 1986. "Making Invisible Women Visible: Studying the History of Muslim Women in South Asia." *South Asia* IX(1): 1–13. doi:10.1080/00856 408608723076.

Mitchell, William J. T. 1987. "The Golden Age of Criticism." *London Review of Books* 9(12).

Moors, Annelies. 2007. "Fashionable Muslims: Notions of Self, Religion and Society in Sana'a." *Fashion Theory: The Journal of Dress, Body, and Culture* 11(2–3): 319–46. doi:10.2752/136270407X202853.

Moore, Raymond A., Jr. 1969. "The Use of the Army in Nation Building: The Case of Pakistan." *Asian Survey* 9(6): 447–56. doi: 10.2307/2642435.

Moreau, Ron, and Michael Hirsh. 2007. "The Most Dangerous Nation in the World isn't Iraq. It's Pakistan". *Newsweek,* October 29.

Moretti, Franco. 2014. *The Bourgeois: Between History and Literature.* London: Verso Books.

Muir, Sarah. 2016. "On Historical Exhaustion: Argentine Critique in an Era of 'Total Corruption.'" *Comparative Studies in Society and History* 58(1):129–58. doi:10.1017/S0010417515000596.

Mumtaz, Kamil K. 1985. *Architecture in Pakistan.* Singapore: Mimar.

Murphy, Richard. 1996. "Space, Class, and Rhetoric in Lahore (unpublished DPhil thesis, University of Oxford).

———. 2000. "The Hairbrush and the Dagger: Mediating Modernity in Lahore." In *Mass Mediations: New Approaches to Popular Culture in the Middle East and Beyond,* edited by Walter Armbrust. Berkeley: University of California Press.

Nasr, Seyyed Vali Reza. 1993. "Islamic Opposition to the Islamic State: The Jama'at-i Islami, 1977–88." *International Journal of Middle East Studies* 25: 261–83. doi:10.1017/S0020743800058529.

———. 1994. *The Vanguard of the Islamic Revolution: The Jam'at-i Islami of Pakistan.* Berkeley: University of California Press.

Navaro-Yashin, Yael. 2002a. "The Market for Identities: Secularism, Islamism, and Commodities." In *Fragments of Culture: The Everyday of Modern Turkey,* edited by Deniz Kandiyoti and Ayse Saktanber. New Brunswick, NJ: Rutgers University Press.

———. 2002b. *Faces of the State: Secularism and Public Life in Turkey.* Princeton, NJ: Princeton University Press.

Nelson, Matthew J. 2009. "Dealing with Difference: Religious Education and the Challenge of Democracy in Pakistan." *Modern Asian Studies* 43(3): 591–618. http://www.jstor.org/stable/20488097.

Nilsson, Sten A. 1973. *The New Capitals of India, Pakistan, and Bangladesh.* Lund, Sweden: Studentlitteratur.

Noman, Omar. 1988. *The Political Economy of Pakistan 1947–1985.* London: Kegan Paul.

Ortner, Sherry B. 1995. "Resistance and the Problem of Ethnographic Refusal." *Comparative Studies in Society and History* 37(1):173–93. http://www.jstor .org/stable/179382.

Osella, Caroline, and Filippo Osella. 2006. "Once upon a Time in the West: Stories of Migration and Modernity from Kerala, South India." *The Journal of the Royal Anthropological Institute* 12: 569–88. doi:10.1111/j.1467-9655 .2006.00353.x.

———. 2008. "Introduction: Islamic Reformism in South Asia." *Modern Asian Studies* 42: 247–257. doi:10.1017/S0026749X07003186.

———. 2008b. "Islamism and Social Reform in Kerala, South India." *Modern Asian Studies* 42: 317–46. doi:10.1017/S0026749X07003198.

———. 2009. "Muslim Entrepreneurs in Public Life between India and the Gulf: Making Good and Doing Good." *The Journal of the Royal Anthropological Institute* 15: 202–21. doi:10.1111/j.1467-9655.2009.01550.x.

Özyürek, Esra. 2004. "Miniaturizing Atatürk: Privatization of State Imagery and Ideology in Turkey." *American Ethnologist* 31(3): 374–91. doi: 10.1525/ae.2004.31.3.374.

———. 2006. *Nostalgia for the Modern: State Secularism and Everyday Politics in Turkey.* Durham, NC: Duke University Press.

Pamük, Orhan. 2008. "Hüzün—Melancholy—Tristesse of Istanbul." In Huyssen, 289–306.

Paracha, Nadeem. 2012. Also Pakistan. *Dawn,* February 9. http://www.dawn.com/news/694239.

Pernau, Margrit. 2013. *Ashraf into Middle Classes: Muslims in Nineteenth Century Delhi.* Delhi: Oxford University Press.

Peters, Emrys. 1976. "From Particularism to Universalism in the Religion of the Cyrenaican Bedouin. *Bulletin* (British Society Middle Eastern Studies) 3(1): 5–14.

Pinault, David. 2008. My Fortune-Telling Parrot Triggers Trouble in Lahore: Street Rituals and the Legacy of Religious Pluralism." In *Notes from the Fortune-telling Parrot: Islam and the Struggle for Religious Pluralism in Pakistan.* London: Equinox.

Preston, Alex. 2015. "At the Karachi Literary Festival, Books Really Are a Matter of Life and Death." *TheGuardian.com,* February 15. https://www.theguardian .com/books/2015/feb/15/karachi-literature-festival-alex-preston-observer.

Pyla, Panayiota. 2008. "Back to the Future: Doxiadis's Plan for Baghdad." *Journal of Planning History* 7(3): 3–19. doi:10.1177/1538513207304697.

Qadeer, Mohammad A. 2015. "Penetrating Insular Walls." *The Friday Times,* April 10. http://www.thefridaytimes.com/tft/penetrating-insular-walls/.

Rahman, Fazlur. 1982. *Islam and Modernity: Transformation of an Intellectual Tradition.* Chicago: University of Chicago Press.

Rashid, Jamil, and Hassan Gardezi, eds. 1983. *Pakistan: Roots of Dictatorship, the Political Economy of a Praetorian State.* London: Zed Books.

Robinson, Francis. 2001. *The 'Ulama of Farangi Mahall and Islamic Culture in South Asia.* London: Hurst.

———. 2004. "Other-Worldly and This-Worldly Islam and the Islamic Revival. A Memorial Lecture for Wilfred Cantwell Smith." *Journal of the Royal Asiatic Society* 14(1): 47–58. http://www.jstor.org/stable/25188432.

Rollier, Paul. 2010. "Texting Islam: Text Messages and Religiosity among Young Pakistanis." *Contemporary South Asia* 18(4): 413–26. doi:10.1080/09584935.2 010.526195.

Roy, Olivier. 1992. *The Failure of Political Islam.* London: Tauris.

———. 2004. *Globalized Islam: The Search for a New Ummah.* London: Hurst.

Salamandra, Christa. 2004. *A New Old Damascus: Authenticity and Distinction in Urban Syria.* Bloomington: Indiana University Press.

Sandıkçı, Özlem, and Guliz Ger. 2001. "Fundamental Fashions: The Cultural Politics of the Turban and the Levi's." *Advances in Consumer Research* 28: 146–50.

———. 2007. "Constructing and Representing an Islamic Consumer in Turkey." *Fashion Theory: The Journal of Dress, Body, and Culture* 11(2–3): 189–210. doi:10.2752/136270407X202754.

Sanyal, Usha. 1999. "The [Re-]construction of South Asian Muslim Identity in Queens, New York." In *The Expanding Landscape: South Asians and the Diaspora,* edited by Carla Petievich. New Delhi: Manohar.

Schielke, Samuli. 2009. "Being Good in Ramadan: Ambivalence, Fragmentation, and the Moral Self in the Lives of Young Egyptians." *The Journal of the Royal Anthropological Institute* 15 (Islam, Politics, Anthropology): 24–S40. doi:10.1111/j.1467–9655.2009.01540.x.

———. 2015. "Living with Unresolved Differences: A Reply to Fadil and Fernando." *Hau* 5(2): 89–92. doi:10.14318/hau5.2.006.

Shah, Bina. 2005. "A Love Affair with Lahore." In *City of Sin and Splendor: Writings on Lahore,* edited by Bapsi Sidhwa. New Delhi: Penguin Books.

Shahzad, Ghaffar. 2009. *Masājid-e-Lahore: Ta'mīr aur jamāliat.* Lahore: Sang-e-Meel.

———. n.d. Māsajid ka tā'mīriātī tasakhus aur martial law. *tārīkh* 3.

Shirazi, Safdar. A., and Syed Jamil Kazmi. 2014. "Analysis of Population Growth and Urban Development in Lahore-Pakistan using Geospatial Techniques: Suggesting Some Future Options." *South Asian Studies* 29(1): 269–280.

Shryock, Andrew. 2002. "New Images of Arab Detroit: Seeing Otherness and Identity through the Lens of September 11." *American Anthropologist* 104(3): 917–22. http://www.jstor.org/stable/3567265.

———. 2004. *Off Stage/On Display: Intimacy and Ethnography in the Age of Public Culture.* Stanford, CA: Stanford University Press.

———. 2008a. "Epilogue on Discipline and Inclusion." In Ewing, 200–206.

———. 2008b. "Ummah and Empire in Detroit: Lessons in Moral Geography."
Paper presented at the Conference on Transnational Discourses of the
Islamic Community, University of Colorado, Boulder, October 24–25.

Siddiqa, Ayesha. 2007. *Military Inc.: Inside Pakistan's Military Economy.* London:
Pluto Press.

Sidhwa, Bapsi. 1988. *Ice Candy Man.* London: Heinemann.

Sikand, Yoginder. 2011. "Islamic Media Mogul Faces New Foes." *The Daily
Times,* February 26.

Sivan, Emmanuel. 1985: *Radical Islam: Medieval Theology and Modern Politics.*
New Haven, CT: Yale University Press.

Soares, Benjamin. 2005. *Islam and the Prayer Economy: History and Authority in a
Malian Town.* Edinburgh: Edinburgh University Press for the International
African Institute.

———, and Filippo Osella. 2009. "Islam, Politics, Anthropology." *The Journal of
the Royal Anthropological Institute* 15 (Islam, Politics, Anthropology): 1-S23.

Spaulding, Frank. 2003. "Ayub Khan, Constantin Doxiadis, and Islamabad:
Biography as Modernity in a Planned Urban Space." In *Pakistan at the
Millennium,* edited by Charles Kennedy, Kathleen McNeil, Carl Ernst, and
David Gilmartin. Oxford: Oxford University Press.

Starrett, Gregory. 1995. "The Political Economy of Religious Commodities in Cairo."
American Anthropologist 97(1): 51–68. doi:10.1525/aa.1995.97.1.02a00090.

———. 1996. "The Margins of Print: Children's Religious Literature in Egypt."
The Journal of the Royal Anthropological Institute 2(1): 117–39.
doi:10.2307/3034636.

———. 1998. *Putting Islam to Work: Education, Politics and Religious
Transformation in Egypt.* Berkeley: University of California Press.

Steinberg, Jonny. 2015. "Why I'm Moving Back to South Africa." *Buzzfeed Books,*
February 18. https://www.buzzfeed.com/jonnysteinberg/why-im-moving-
back-to-south-africa?utm_term=.ylelzGbnE#.odbQPVvk9.

Still, Clarinda. 2011. "Spoiled Brides and the Fear of Education: Honor and
Social Mobility among Dalits in South India." *Modern Asian Studies* 45(5):
1119–46. doi: 10.1017/S0026749X10000144.

Swartz, David. 1997. *Culture and Power: The Sociology of Pierre Bourdieu.* Chicago:
University of Chicago Press.

Talbot, Ian. 1996. *Khizr Tiwana: The Punjab Unionist Party and the Partition of
India.* Surrey, UK: Curzon.

———. 1998. *Pakistan: A Modern History.* London: Hurst.

———. 2006. *Divided Cities: Partition and Its Aftermath in Lahore and Amritsar,
1947–1957.* Karachi: Oxford University Press.

Tallis, Raymond. 1995. "The Survival of Theory: Overstanding the Text." *P.N. Review* 101 21(3): 36–39.

———. 2008. License My Roving Hands: "Does Neuroscience Really have Anything to Teach us About the Pleasure of Reading John Donne?". *Times Literary Supplement*, February 11: 13-15.

Tarlo, Emma. 2010. *Visibly Muslim: Politics, Fashion, Faith.* Oxford: Oxford University Press.

Tavernese, Sabrina. 2010. "Mystical Form of Islam Suits Sufis in Pakistan." *New York Times,* February 25. http://www.nytimes.com/2010/02/26/world /worldspecial/26lahore.html?_r=0

Toor, Saadia. 2011. *The State of Islam: Culture and Cold War Politics in Pakistan.* London: Pluto Press.

Wacquant, Loic. 2012. "Three Steps to a Historical Anthropology of Actually Existing Neoliberalism." *Social Anthropology/Anthropology Sociale* 20(1): 66–79. doi: 10.1111/j.1469–8676.2011.00189.x.

Watkins, Francis. 2009. "'God Don't Kill the Traveller, Grant Their Desire That Their Last Breath Be at Home': An Analysis of Pakhtun Migrants' Tales." In *Pakistani Diasporas: Culture, Conflict and Change,* edited by Virinder Kalra. Karachi: Oxford University Press.

Wilk, Richard. 1995. "Learning to be Local in Belize: Global Systems of Common Difference." In *Worlds Apart: Modernity through the Prism of the Local,* edited by Daniel Miller. London: Routledge.

Yaqin, Amina. 2007. "Islamic Barbie: The Politics of Gender and Peformativity." *Fashion Theory: The Journal of Dress, Body, and Culture* 11(2–3): 173–88. doi:10.2752/136270407X202736.

Zaman, Qasim M. 2002. *The Ulama in Contemporary Islam: Custodians of Change.* Princeton, NJ: Princeton University Press.

Zamindar, V. Fazila-Yacoobali. 2007. *The Long Partition and the Making of Modern South Asia.* Columbia, NY: Columbia University Press.

INFORMANT INTERVIEWS AND DISCUSSIONS

Pseudonyms have been used to protect the confidentiality and privacy of all informants. The only exception to this are interviews with military officials and individuals in prominent positions, where withholding names will not ensure anonymization.

Abeer Taimur [pseud.], in discussion with author, February 1, 2009.

Afifa Omar [pseud.], in discussion with author, December 19, 2013.

Afshan Attique [pseud.], in discussion with author, March 13, 2010.

Ahmad Kamal [pseud.], in discussion with author, January 1, 2010.
Ahmed Khan [pseud.], in discussion with author, October 23, 2009.
Ahmed Qureshi [pseud.], in discussion with author, March 3, 2014.
Amina Ahsan [pseud.], in discussion with author, September 5 and October 5, 2009.
———, in a *dars* at her residence, March 7, 2010.
Annie Alvi [pseud.], in discussion with author, January 4, 2010.
Ayesha Ansari [pseud.], in discussion with author, October 29, 2009.
Ayesha Khan [pseud.], in discussion with author, September 27, 2009.
Ayesha Nisar [pseud.], in a speech at a student hostel, August 28, 2009.
Chanda Chugtai [pseud.], in discussion with author, October 1 and 20, 2009, and March 23, 2010.
Ejaz Haider (former editor of *The Daily Times*), in discussion with author, May 4, 2010.
Farah Azhar [pseud.], in discussion with author, September 27, 2009.
Fareeha Jamshed [pseud.], in discussion with author, November 24, 2009.
Farida Amir [pseud.], in discussion with author, October 13, 2010.
Fatima Hamid [pseud.], in discussion with author, December 1, 2013.
Haroon Ghafoor [pseud.], in interview with author, April 3, 2010.
Hasan Mahmood [pseud.], in discussion with author, September 26, 2009.
Iqbal Zaki [pseud.], in discussion with author, December 12, 2009.
Jamshed Ahmed [pseud.], in discussion with author, January 9, 2010.
Kamil Khan Mumtaz (principal architect at KKM Architects), in interview with author, December 5, 2009.
Leena Raza [pseud.], in discussion with author, January 4, 2010.
Mahnaz Hussain [pseud.], in discussion with the author, July 23, 2009.
Mariyam Zaman [pseud.], in discussion with author, August 1, 2010.
Mehreen Ali [pseud.], in discussion with author, April 4, 2010.
Mohammad Karim [pseud.], in discussion with author, October 28, 2009.
Muhammad Aslam Rana (brigadier, administrator, Defence Housing Authority, Lahore), in interview with author, October 10, 2009.
Mujib-ur-Rehman [pseud.], in interview with author, February 9, 2010.
Nasira Waheed [pseud.], in interview with author, February 20, 2010.
Nina Khan, [pseud.] discussion with author, September 27, 2009.
Nuzhat Saleem [pseud.], in discussion with author, August 9 and September 12, 2009.
Qasim Butt [pseud.], in discussion with author, October 3, 3009.
Rashid Jatt [pseud.], in discussion with author, September 26, 2009.
Rahat Cheema [pseud.], in discussion with author, April 29, 2010.
Rehana Karamat [pseud.], in discussion with author, December 5, 2013.

Rubina Farhan [pseud.], in discussion with author, November 15, 2009.

Saima Abbas [pseud.], in discussion with author, March 13, 2010.

Sajida Wasti [pseud.], in discussion with author, February 1, 2009, and March 13, 2010.

Samina Rahman [pseud.], in discussion with author, September 29, 2009.

Samra Shaukat [pseud.] in, discussion with author, December 17, 2009.

Seema Rahim [pseud.], in discussion with author, January 4, 2010.

Shahid Hussain [pseud.], in discussion with author, February 13, 2010.

Shahid Manzoor [pseud.], in discussion with author, March 12, 2010.

Shaista Rahman [pseud.], in discussion with author, July 12, 2009.

Taimur Jibran [pseud.], in discussion with author, March 23 and April 4, 2009.

Yaqoob Khalili [pseud.], in discussion with author, September 17, 2009.

Acknowledgments

The debts I have accumulated since the inception of this project can only be acknowledged but never repaid. The biggest of these debts are to the women and men who form the subject material of the book. As a Pakistani brought up in relatively privileged and largely secular circles, I was immersed in the narratives of the progressive middle class of the country. I am immensely grateful to all my informants for shaking that certainty—as unsettling as it was—and for pushing me to rethink what I thought I knew. At Harvard University Press, I greatly appreciate the enduring interest and support of Sharmila Sen, as well as Heather Hughes's diligence and patience in shepherding the project to completion.

My deepest gratitude goes to Paul Dresch, who introduced me to the discipline of anthropology. All of us who have been taught by Paul know that it is a privilege to be under his supervision. I am also thankful to Robert Parkin for his advice throughout the writing process. An earlier version of this manuscript benefited immensely from the careful reading and commentary of Anatol Lieven and Morgan Clarke, and I am grateful for their continued involvement as I reworked the original draft. In addition, the book arrived at its current form through the very insightful feedback of two anonymous reviewers. I am grateful to Kamran Asdar Ali for taking time to discuss parts of the argument with me. Humeira Iqtidar and Amina Yaqin have provided invaluable counsel on many of the themes within the book. Ali Khan has had no choice except to be supportive, especially since it was his encouragement that led me to graduate studies in anthropology. I received financial support from the Higher Education Commission, Pakistan, along with several grants from Magdalen College, Oxford, and a writing-up bursary from the Institute of Social and Cultural Anthropology, Oxford. This book was written with the support of an ESRC Future Research Leaders Fellowship at the Institute of Social and Cultural Anthropology and a Junior Research Fellowship at St. Catherine's College, Oxford.

I would like to thank my colleagues in the Anthropology of Religion Reading Group at Oxford for creating a warm and constructive space for discussion. In particular, I am grateful to Giulia Liberatore for her careful reading and for initiating an intellectual partnership that I hope will continue to flourish. Various parts of this book were presented at the University of Chicago, the University of Edinburgh, SOAS University of London, and the University of California, Berkeley, as well as at the Association of Asian Studies Annual Conference (Toronto, 2012) and the Association of Social Anthropologist Annual Conference (Edinburgh, 2014). Elements of the arguments developed in Chapter 4 of this book were initially examined in an earlier article in *Cultural Studies*, titled "'Buying Modern': Muslim Subjectivity, the West and Patterns of Islamic Consumption in Lahore, Pakistan" (28[1]: 84–107).

I am fortunate to have friends with whom I could share both the fruits and the burdens of the writing process. I want to thank Radhika Gupta, Laia Soto Bermant, Tomohiro Morisawa, Ivan Costantino, Stephen Robertson, and Moizza Binat Sarwar for their camaraderie and support. Maryam Wasif has been an ever-constant source of transliteration and gastronomical advice. The inevitable lows of writing were made infinitely better by the indulgent generosity of Tehniyet Kardar and Osman Chaudry, and by the Lahori-style hospitality of Susannah Harris-Wilson. I played an integral role in sealing Umal Azmat's professional fate and, in turn, she has supported my equally dubious, career choices. During the various stages of writing, rewriting, and revisions, my *langoṭia* from home, Mina Malik-Hussain and Amena Raja, have remained close at hand and heart. My friends from London, Hiba Sameen and Fizza Husain, have never let me feel far from home. Most of all, I am indebted to Leslie Fesenmyer, Iza Kavedžija, and Ayesha Siddiqi for their friendship and presence when I needed it most.

I have been humbled by the support I received from my family. At the risk of sounding like a poor version of a well-known Pakistani bumper sticker, I firmly believe that none of this would have been possible without the love of my mother, Nishat Maqsood. Both my siblings, Huma Maqsood and Saad Maqsood, and my "other sibling," Maryam Wazirzada, have been by my side, always ready to cheer me on. I am especially grateful to Mary Eagleton for going beyond the call of usual mother-in-law duties in reading and rereading manuscript drafts, and my father-in-law, David Pierce, for his support at every step in the journey. My husband, Matthew Eagleton-Pierce, treated this book as a labor of love. The immenseness of his generosity and patience render words of thanks trivial.

My father, Humayun Maqsood, passed away while I was working on this book. It is to him that this book is dedicated. Never that keen on traveling abroad, he had told me—in what became our last conversation—that he was looking forward to coming to my book launch. The relief that I feel at finally finishing a project so close to his heart is anchored in the sadness of his absence. I can only hope that this is a book he would have been proud of. Any errors contained within are, of course, entirely my own.

Index